Exercises in applied genetics

Exercises in applied genetics

Lynn Burnet

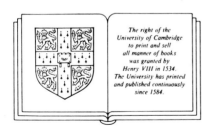

The right of the
University of Cambridge
to print and sell
all manner of books
was granted by
Henry VIII in 1534.
The University has printed
and published continuously
since 1584.

CAMBRIDGE UNIVERSITY PRESS

Cambridge

New York   New Rochelle   Melbourne   Sydney

The publishers would like to thank the following for supplying photographs:
Figure 5.1 Professor Hussey, John Innes Institute
Figure 5.2a Dr W. A. Lawrence, John Innes Institute
Figure 5.2b Dr J. Watts, John Innes Institute
Figure 5.4 Professor F. Caro, Science Photo Library
Figure 6.1 Dr A. J. Jeffreys, University of Leicester, reprinted by permission from *Nature* Vol. 316 pp. 76–79, Fig. 2 copyright © 1985 Macmillan Magazines Ltd.
Figure 6.5.1 Centre for Human Genetics, University of Sheffield
Figure 6.7.1 Muscular Dystrophy Group of Great Britain and Northern Ireland

The publishers would also like to thank the following for permission to redraw illustrations:
Figure 2.4.1 from Wriedt, C. (1930),
Heredity in Livestock, Macmillan, London.
Figure 2.4.2 from Lush, J. L. (1951),
Genetics in the 20th Century Ed. L. C. Dunn,
Macmillan, New York.
Figure 2.5.1 and **6.2a** from *Modern Genetics* by F. J. Ayala and J. A. Kiger 1984 Benjamin Cummings Publishing Co. Inc.
Figure 5.4.1 from *Principles of Gene Manipulation* by R. W. Old and S. B. Primrose 1985 Blackwells Scientific Publications Ltd
Figure 6.2b from *The New Genetics and Clinical Practice* by D. J. Weatherall 2/e Published by Oxford University Press 1986 © Oxford University Press 1986

Published by the Press Syndicate of the University of Cambridge
The Pitt Building, Trumpington Street, Cambridge CB2 1RP
32 East 57th Street, New York, NY 10022, USA
10 Stamford Road, Oakleigh, Melbourne 3166, Australia

First published 1988

Printed in Great Britain by Scotprint, Musselburgh, Scotland

British Library cataloguing in publication data
Burnet, Lynn
  Exercises in applied genetics.
  1. Genetics
  I. Title
  575.1   QH430

ISBN 0 521 33883 2

Contents

Preface

This book has arisen out of a recognition of the need for source material in teaching aspects of genetics which relate to such topics as animal and plant production, pest and disease control, and medicine. The approach adopted is designed to involve students in active learning.

The exercises provide practice in problem solving in the areas specified in GCE Advanced Level syllabuses featuring applied genetics. The level of knowledge assumed is a basic grounding in Mendelian genetics, such as may be acquired from the companion volume *Essential Genetics*, as well as an appreciation of the structure and function of nucleic acids. The exercises in the present volume are versatile in that many of the problems are sufficiently open-ended also to provide a challenge for post A-level students. University and college lecturers may find useful material for undergraduate tutorials here.

The book is intended not just to impart information but also to provoke discussion and the exchange of ideas. To this end, the exercises have been devised as learning situations in which students and teachers work collaboratively. Teachers should appreciate that A-level students will find some of the problems too difficult to tackle without assistance. The purpose of the exercises is to stimulate curiosity and active participation.

The material follows a logical progression and, to a certain extent, later exercises build on concepts introduced in earlier sections. However, if the book is to be used as a text to accompany a course in applied genetics, it is not necessary to work through the chapters in order. There are cross-references throughout to help with the planning of a teaching programme.

The answers provided are at the depth required of an A-level student while undergraduates might be expected also to identify and explore associated problems. Suggested reading, notes and sources are included to assist with points raised in discussion and with follow-up work.

Acknowledgements

Much of the preliminary research for this book was carried out at Cambridge University while I was a Schoolteacher Fellow Commoner. I am most grateful to the Master and Fellows of St Catharine's College, Cambridge, for providing this opportunity. This period was also made possible by the Goldsmiths' Company who generously provided financial support and the City of Sheffield Education Department who granted a term's secondment.

I wish to thank Professor H. W. Woolhouse, Director of the John Innes Institute, Norwich, for permission to use the Institute's library and Professor J. A. Roper for permission to use the reference collection in the Department of Genetics, University of Sheffield.

I would also like to express my appreciation to those who read and commented on the manuscript, Drs Barrie Burnet, Diana Curtis, Trevor Elkington, Morris Grindle, Bryan Howard, Angela Stafford and Peter Sudbery of the University of Sheffield, and Drs John Barrett and Philip Greig. I am indebted to my husband for his suggestions and criticisms and for testing many of the exercises in undergraduate tutorials. Finally, thanks are due to David and Laurence Winston who provided their fingerprints for figure 1.2.1 and to the sixth-form pupils at King Edward VII School, Sheffield, for their comments on some of the problems.

ANDREA HASTINGS.

"Some would blame your genes. Others would blame your environment, but I blame you, Jason. I blame you."

1 Introduction to quantitative genetics

Introduction

Genetics is a fundamental biological science. Its origins lie in attempts to understand why offspring resemble their parents and the associated desire to breed certain qualities into domestic animals and plants. It has therefore been an 'applied science' from its beginning. Although the science of genetics has grown into a highly academic discipline, it continues to have important practical applications.

Gregor Mendel, in his famous experiments with the garden pea, discovered consistency in heredity where others had failed, because he concentrated on a single character at a time and followed his breeding experiments through several generations. Mendel published his conclusions concerning heredity in peas in 1866 and later worked on heredity in other plant species but his work did not become widely known in his lifetime. Attention was drawn to Mendel's work in 1900 by Carl Correns, Erich von Tschermak and Hugo de Vries. It was de Vries and Correns who explicitly stated the principles discovered by Mendel; the only law that Mendel himself stated was the one we now call his second law. They pointed out that the principle of segregation is implicit in the law of independent assortment so we now speak of Mendel's first law as the **Law of Segregation** and his second law as the **Law of Independent Assortment** although he himself did not make this distinction. Mendel and his rediscoverers were able to recognise the important principle of segregation because the characters with which they worked were inherited in an uncomplicated way; the alternative traits were distinct and were controlled by just one pair of alleles.

Most characters of economic importance such as milk yield, rate of growth and egg laying capacity are measurable, **quantitative characters** showing **continuous variation** (exercise 1.1). It was not immediately obvious how Mendelian principles might be applied to these characters until the experiments of **Nilsson-Ehle** showed how segregation can explain the inheritance of continuous variation too (exercise 1.2).

One of the chief problems in analysing continuous variation is to discover how much of the variation between individuals is due to the effects of genes and how much is due to environmental differences (exercise 1.3). For instance, the colour of the cream (butterfat) on milk is more yellow in some breeds of cattle (e.g. Jersey and Guernsey) than in others, but the colour also depends on the diet of the cow. The yellow colour is derived from carotenes in green foods so the cream may be white because the cow has not fed on green food or because she has enzymes in the liver which break down carotenes. Qualitative, discontinuously varying characters are also affected by the environment but it remains possible to distinguish genotypes from their phenotypes.

Quantitative, continuously varying characters are under the control of many genes; they are **polygenically** controlled (poly = many). Quantitative characters are much more susceptible to environmental modification than are qualitative ones and this makes it virtually impossible to ascertain an individual's genotype from observation of its phenotype. It is important to know how much of the phenotypic variation is due to genetic differences between individuals because only genetic variation is inherited. Breeders use statistical methods to analyse the sources of variation and therefore to discover how far the character might be improved by selection. Some of the methods of quantitative genetics are introduced in the following exercises.

1.1 Genetic basis of continuous variation

Geneticists often choose to work on the inheritance of characters which have clearly distinguishable forms or traits where every individual falls into one category or another and there are no intermediates. This kind of variation is described as **discontinuous** and it is from the study of inheritance of such characters that Mendelian principles are learned and taught. However, most characters of economic importance are not classifiable in this way. Variation extending from a low to a high value with every value in between can be seen in such characters as milk production, egg laying, wool quality and the number of offspring in a litter. There is variation in degree rather than in kind. An individual's phenotype is measurable (quantifiable) and does not fit into one discrete category or another but falls somewhere on a continuous range. These characters are therefore said to show **continuous variation**. The terms continuous and discontinuous describe the type of *phenotypic* variation in a population. Examples of continuous variation are illustrated in figure 1.1.1.

Figure 1.1.1(a) shows the distribution of corneal diameter with a smooth curve connecting the midpoints of the column tops. This bell-shaped curve is called a **normal distribution** or **normal curve**. In a normal distribution, most individuals cluster about a most frequent class which is called the **mode**. The normal distribution has a single peak and is called **unimodal**. If there is clustering

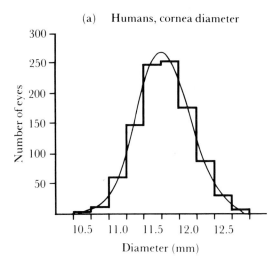

Figure 1.1.1 *Continuous variation*

(a)   Humans, cornea diameter

(b)   Rice, spikelet length

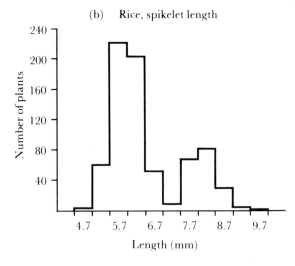

about two modes, as in figure 1.1.1(b), the distribution is **bimodal**.

Genetically determined discontinuous phenotypic variation is often due to the segregation of one or two pairs of alleles. Variation in continuous characters may be explained by the simultaneous segregation of more than two pairs of alleles. One of the first investigations into the genetic control of continuous variation is that of Nilsson-Ehle, a Swedish plant breeder. He made crosses between pure breeding red and white seeded wheat plants.

1 Variety A (white seeds) was crossed to variety B (red seeds) and the F_1 plants were allowed to self-fertilise to obtain the F_2. The F_1 generation had intermediate red seeds and the F_2 plants were in the ratio 1 red : 2 intermediate red : 1 white.
   (a) How many gene loci control the difference in seed colour between strains A and B?
   (b) Define gene symbols and suggest genotypes for the F_2 plants.

2 Two gene loci determine the difference in seed colour between another white seeded and red seeded variety of wheat. The white variety has the genotype $w^1w^1\,y^1y^1$ and the red variety has the genotype $w^2w^2\,y^2y^2$. Each w^2 and y^2 allele increases the intensity of colour of the seeds by a small amount, giving four possible degrees of intensity of red as well as white in the F_2 progeny. What would be the ratio of these five phenotypes in an F_2 generation derived from the red and white seeded plants? (Use a Punnett square to find the genotypes.)

3 Nilsson-Ehle demonstrated that two of his wheat varieties differed by three gene loci all affecting the colour of the seeds. Let the genotype of the white seeded parent be represented ⚬⚬⚬. Let the genotype of the red seeded parent be represented ●●●. Then the genotype of the F_1 generation is represented ●●●.

The eight possible kinds of male and female gametes from the F_1 plants are shown in the margins of figure 1.1.2. Copy this figure and write in the boxes the number of 'red genes' in each zygote.

4 Using the data in the completed table, plot a histogram with frequency of zygotes on the vertical axis and number of 'red genes' on the horizontal axis.

5 Suppose the presence of each 'red gene' in the genotype adds a certain amount of red to the phenotype. How many shades of red should be distinguishable in the F_2 progeny?

This population of F_2 plants shows continuous variation from the darkest red to white with the intermediate shades being the most frequent. This phenotypic distribution is a consequence of segregation of two incompletely dominant alleles at each of three gene loci.

Further studies like Nilsson-Ehle's have confirmed that continuous phenotypic variation can be partly explained by the simultaneous segregation of alleles at many gene loci, each gene having a small effect. Characters controlled in this way are said to show **polygenic** (or **multifactorial**) inheritance and the genes involved are called **polygenes**. This exercise has demonstrated that the number of loci involved may be as few as three. If there is incomplete dominance such that each allele makes a contribution to the phenotypic value, the number of grades of phenotype increases as the number of gene loci increases.

It is not essential that the allele pairs show incomplete dominance (or act additively, see exercise 1.5). Figure 1.1.3 shows the expected distribution of grades of phenotype where the character is affected by six gene loci with one dominant and one recessive allele at each locus. The distribution represented is that expected in an F_2 generation derived from an

Figure 1.1.2 *Punnett square showing possible combinations of gametes carrying three genes for seed colour.*

Gametes	●●●	●●⚬	●⚬●	⚬●●	⚬⚬●	⚬●⚬	●⚬⚬	⚬⚬⚬
●●●								
●●⚬								
●⚬●								
⚬●●								
⚬●⚬								
⚬●⚬								
●⚬⚬								
⚬⚬⚬								

Figure 1.1.3 *Distribution of grades of phenotype expected in an F$_2$ generation where six gene loci affect the character, with complete dominance at each gene locus*

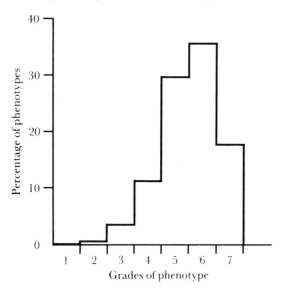

Grades of phenotype

F$_1$ generation heterozygous at each of the six gene loci.

Polygenes do not necessarily have an equal magnitude of effect. In Friesian cattle for instance, several gene loci affect the colouring of the coat. One of them, which may be called a major gene, determines whether or not there are any white markings. If the animal is homozygous recessive at this locus the extent of the white marking is controlled by a series of other modifier genes (polygenes). A further example of a major gene with modifiers is given in exercise 3.5. The distinction between major gene and polygene is only for convenience of description; they grade into each other in the magnitude of their effect on the phenotype and there is no physical difference between them.

1.2 *Environmental variation*

It would be a mistake to think that all differences between individuals are a consequence of differences in genotype. Genes determine the direction of development but the environment provides the physical space and the raw materials, so the phenotype of any organism is a result of interaction between its genotype and its environment. For example, human monozygotic (identical) twins which have developed from the same fertilised egg and have shared the same uterus are not identical in every respect even at birth, and as they grow to adulthood, individual experiences make each one unique despite the identity of genotype.

1 Say whether you think the following aspects of the phenotypes of monozygotic twins are almost certainly identical or not necessarily identical:
(i) accent, (ii) blood group, (iii) personality, (iv) eye colour, (v) hair colour, (vi) weight, (vii) height, (viii) skin colour, (ix) length of fingernails, (x) fingerprints (see figure 1.2.1).

Environmental influences are very important in characters of economic importance such as

Figure 1.2.1   *Fingerprints of monozygotic twins*

David, thumb   Laurence, thumb

David, little finger   Laurence, little finger

the weight of a lamb at a certain age. The growth of the lamb will be affected by the state of health and level of nutrition of its mother both before birth and while it is suckling, and whether there is competition with siblings (brothers and sisters). Freedom from parasites and disease has a beneficial effect on growth while climatic conditions are important in that the more energy which is used for maintenance of body temperature, the less is available for growth.

Much of the variation in quantitative characters is environmentally determined but the expression of major genes too can be modified by environmental factors.

2 (a) It is possible to make some homozygous recessive dwarf varieties of plants such as peas and corn grow to normal size by treating them with gibberellic acid. A dwarf pea plant was treated in this way and allowed to self-fertilise. What would be the phenotype of its untreated progeny?

(b) A pure breeding variety of dwarf plant was treated with gibberellic acid for six generations so that in each generation, all the plants were phenotypically tall. The seventh generation was not treated. What would be the phenotype of these plants?

3 Refer to exercise 1.1, figure 1.1.1(b). This is a graph showing the distribution of phenotypes in an F_2 generation. Assume that mean spikelet length is controlled by a single gene locus and the F_1 plants were heterozygous at this locus. Explain the shape of the histogram in figure 1.1.1(b).

Johannsen, a Danish geneticist, performed a series of experiments to investigate the causes of variation in the weight of bean seeds. He obtained several kilograms of beans from a commercial grower and found that their sizes ranged from 150 mg to 900 mg. All of these beans would have come from many different plants but as they are normally self-fertilising

it can be assumed that each bean was homozygous at almost all of its gene loci. Johannsen chose 19 seeds ranging from light to heavy, planted them all under the same environmental conditions and collected the seeds produced by each plant separately. A few seeds from each family were sown the next year and the progeny were harvested. In this way Johannsen obtained 19 separate groups of seeds derived from the original 19 beans. Each group of beans would be homozygous at almost all gene loci and each group is called a **pure line**. Table 1.2.1 shows the variation in seed weight in line 1 and line 19.

Table 1.2.1 *Variation in seed weight in two pure lines*

Weight of seed in mg	Number of seeds	
	Line 1	Line 19
100–150	0	4
150–200	0	4
200–250	0	5
250–300	0	19
300–350	0	69
350–400	2	69
400–450	5	44
450–500	9	5
500–550	14	0
550–600	21	0
600–650	22	0
650–700	24	0
700–750	23	0
750–800	17	0
800–850	6	0
850–900	2	0

4 Using the data in table 1.2.1 plot histograms of the variation in seed weight in line 1 and in line 19.

5 The mean weight of seeds in line 1 is 642 mg and that in line 19 is 351 mg. What is the cause of this difference between the means?

6 What is the cause of the variation in seed weight within line 1 and within line 19?

7 (a) If the two seeds in line 1 which weighed between 350 and 400 mg were sown, what would you expect the mean weight of their progeny to be?

(b) If the two seeds in line 1 which weighed between 850 and 900 mg were sown, what would you expect the mean weight of their progeny to be? Explain your answers.

8 (a) Table 1.2.2 shows the range of variation found in three more of Johannsen's pure lines. Using the data in the column headed 'Total', plot a histogram illustrating the variation in the whole population of beans.

(b) What are the causes of variation in the whole population?

(c) In the progeny from the heaviest seed in this population, what would you expect the maximum and minimum seed weights to be?

(d) If you took a seed in the 400–450 mg class in the histogram you have plotted, what range of variation might you expect in its progeny?

Some populations of domesticated species are like Johannsen's pure lines, i.e. all the individuals are homozygous and genetically identical. Varieties of wheat provide good examples of pure lines, where all the observed variation between plants within a variety is due to **environmental factors**. All sheep or cows belonging to a particular breed resemble each other because they have certain genes in common but they cannot be considered 'pure lines' because they are neither homozygous at all loci nor are all individuals genetically identical. Variation between animals in a flock or herd is due to both **genetic and environmental** differences. For the breeder, knowledge of how much of the observed variation is genetic in origin will give him or her some idea of how successful a programme of selection might be. Environmental variation is not inherited. Within each of Johannsen's pure lines, the seeds are genetically identical, so the biggest seeds will pass on the same genes to the next generation as will the smallest seeds and there will be no change in the average phenotype. There must be genetic differences between individuals if selection is to bring about change over subsequent generations.

Table 1.2.2   *Variation in seed weight in three pure lines*

Weight of seeds in mg	Line 3	Line 11	Line 18	Total
100–150	0	0	1	1
150–200	0	1	3	4
200–250	0	2	11	13
250–300	0	14	22	36
300–350	0	38	29	67
350–400	5	104	72	181
400–450	14	172	120	306
450–500	50	179	69	298
500–550	76	140	23	239
550–600	58	53	5	116
600–650	44	9	2	55
650–700	29	0	0	29
700–750	5	0	0	5
750–800	1	0	0	1

1.3 Inbreeding and outbreeding

Mating with a genetically related partner is called **inbreeding** and the most extreme form is **self-fertilisation**. Some cultivated plants such as cotton, oats, peas, tomatoes and wheat are normally self-fertilising and many commercial varieties of these plants are pure lines (i.e. all plants are genetically identical and homozygous at most gene loci). Plants within a line will show some environmental variation, but if they are grown in similar conditions, they will have a phenotypic uniformity which is of considerable importance to the grower; profits are greater when all the produce is of a similar high quality, and cultivation and harvesting are made easier if the plants are synchronised in their growth. Another benefit of homozygosity at almost all gene loci is that future generations will inherit the same genotype, i.e. the variety will **breed true**.

1 Inbreeding tends to result in homozygosity at most gene loci. Consider just one gene locus in a self-fertilising species of plant. The F_1 progeny of a plant with the genotype *Aa* are represented by figure 1.3.1. The shaded portion is the proportion of the progeny which are homozygotes (both *AA* and *aa*).

Figure 1.3.1 *Proportion of homozygotes and heterozygotes in the progeny of a self-fertilised plant with genotype Aa*

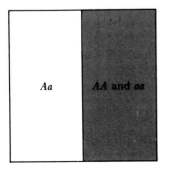

(a) These offspring reproduce by self-fertilisation. The *AA* and *aa* homozygotes produce homozygotes like themselves. What fraction of the progeny from the heterozygotes will be homozygous?

(b) An F_2 generation is derived by allowing all of the F_1 generation to self-fertilise. Copy figure 1.3.1, making the sides 4 cm long. The square now represents the whole of the F_2 generation. Colour in an appropriate portion of the white section to represent the increase in homozygosity in this second generation of inbreeding.

(c) What fraction of the population will be heterozygous in the fourth generation of inbreeding?

If a cross is made artificially between two varieties of a normally self-fertilising species like the garden pea, a large number of loci affecting many aspects of the phenotype will be made heterozygous. When the plants are allowed to self-fertilise in subsequent generations, each locus will tend to become homozygous for one allele as illustrated in question 1, but all the plants will not become homozygous for the same alleles. In order to make a pure line therefore, the breeder selects a small number of desirable plants, grows the progeny of each plant separately and selects again. This is continued until the selected line is sufficiently homozygous to breed true. When a particular allele is homozygous in every individual in a population we say that the allele has been **fixed**.

2 Two inbred varieties of plant, genotypes *AA bb cc DD EE ff* and *aa BB cc dd EE FF* are crossed.
(a) What will be the genotype of the F_1 hybrid produced as a result of crossing these two plants?
(b) If the F_1 hybrids and subsequent generations are selfed until all loci are

again homozygous, how many different pure lines could be produced?

Compared with the growing of plants, keeping animals is more costly in time and space as well as money so it is more difficult to maintain a large population from which to select animals for breeding purposes. Inbreeding increases the number of homozygous loci but there is no control over which alleles are becoming fixed and fixation of harmful alleles can be a problem when there is only a small breeding population. In general, populations of animals and cross-fertilising plants carry in the heterozygous state, recessive alleles having deleterious (harmful) effects on reproductive capacity. In normally self-fertilising species recessive alleles causing a decrease in fitness will quickly become homozygous and will tend to be eliminated from the population by natural selection. But in a cross-fertilising (**outbreeding**) population where there is a high level of heterozygosity, any such deleterious alleles will be able to reach quite a high frequency in the gene pool before many homozygotes appear. Mating between close relations in a normally outbreeding population increases the likelihood that deleterious recessive alleles will become homozygous.

3 What do you understand by the gene pool of a population?

4 Cystic fibrosis is a disease in humans caused by a recessive allele. Affected individuals are homozygous while heterozygotes are phenotypically normal. In Europeans the frequency of cystic fibrosis is about one in 2500 births.
  (a) Using the Hardy–Weinberg formula, calculate the frequency of the allele for cystic fibrosis amongst Europeans.
  (b) Approximately what percentage of the European population is heterozygous for the allele?

Crossing the two parental varieties of animal or plant and selecting amongst their offspring is a way of producing new varieties which exceed either parental type in some aspect of the phenotype.

5 In the cross given in question 2,
  $AA\,bb\,cc\,DD\,EE\,ff$ × $aa\,BB\,cc\,dd\,EE\,FF$,
  let each capital letter represent a dominant allele and each small letter represent a recessive allele. Let the six gene loci affect the number of flowers produced by the plant. All the homozygous recessive loci reduce the number of flowers from the maximum possible. Give the genotype of the pure line derived from this cross which would have

  (a) the maximum number of flowers,

  (b) the minimum number of flowers.

Flower number is associated with reproductive capacity so in selecting for increased number, the breeder may expect to increase the fitness of the selected lines. However, if a farmer is selecting to improve a character such as wool quality in sheep, recessive alleles with a deleterious effect on fertility may be accumulating. It is possible that such undesirable genes are linked to genes for wool quality, making it difficult to improve the wool without reducing the fertility of the breed.

It is frequently found that **inbred lines** (breeds or varieties with a history of inbreeding), and especially those derived from normally outbred species, produce fewer offspring than varieties having a high degree of heterozygosity. Inbred animals and plants are also often inferior in terms of size, length of life and resistance to infection. This reduction in fitness is called **inbreeding depression**. In the farmer's desire for uniformity of phenotype within a crop or breed of animal and from one generation to the next, a certain amount of inbreeding depression must often be tolerated.

1.4 *Measuring variation*

East and Hayes crossed two highly inbred varieties of maize (corn), Tom Thumb and Black Mexican, which differed in the length of the cob. The resulting F_1 plants were inter-crossed to produce an F_2 generation. Figure 1.4.1 shows the lengths of the cobs in the two parental varieties, the F_1 and the F_2.

1 (a) If Tom Thumb and Black Mexican are homozygous at all loci affecting cob

Figure 1.4.1 *Length of cobs in two inbred varieties of maize and the F_1 and F_2 generations*

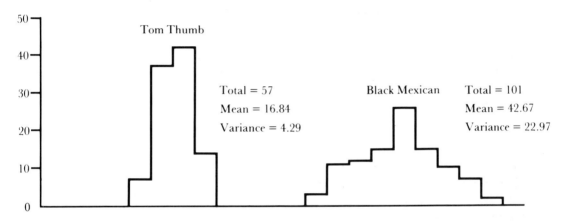

Tom Thumb

Total = 57
Mean = 16.84
Variance = 4.29

Black Mexican   Total = 101
Mean = 42.67
Variance = 22.97

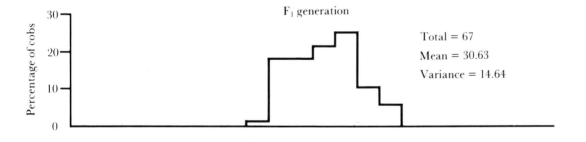

F_1 generation

Total = 67
Mean = 30.63
Variance = 14.64

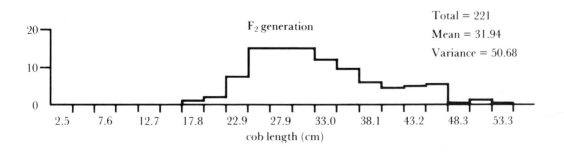

F_2 generation

Total = 221
Mean = 31.94
Variance = 50.68

Percentage of cobs

cob length (cm)

length, what is the cause of the phenotypic variation within the Tom Thumb and within the Black Mexican varieties?

(b) If Tom Thumb has the genotype *aa bb cc dd ee* and Black Mexican has the genotype a^1a^1 b^1b^1 c^1c^1 d^1d^1 e^1e^1 what is the genotype of the F_1 plants?

(c) What is the cause of the phenotypic variation in the F_1 generation?

(d) Considering loci 'A' and 'B' only, how many genotypes are possible in the F_2 generation?

(e) What are the causes of the phenotypic variation in the F_2 generation?

The mean cob lengths (figure 1.4.1) of the F_1 and F_2 generations are very similar and fall between the means for the two parental generations but the spread around the mean is much greater in the F_2 than in the F_1 generation. This variation can be expressed as a statistic called the **variance** which is given for each generation in figure 1.4.1. The largest variance occurs in the F_2 generation because here it has two components while the variance within the parental and F_1 lines has only one component (see questions 1a, 1c and 1e above). It is possible to get an estimate of how much of the variance in the F_2 generation is genetic in origin by subtraction.

2 The environmental component of the variance is called V_E. Use the values for variances given in figure 1.4.1 and your answers to parts of question 1 and calculate the mean value for V_E.

3 The phenotypic variation V_P in the F_2 population is both environmental and genetic in origin ($V_E + V_G$). Calculate V_G.

Selection for improvement in a character will be effective only if there is some genetic component to the observed phenotypic variation... ~~because~~ environmental variation is not
inherited... ~~ortion of the total varia-~~

tion in a character which is genetic in origin gives the breeder some idea of how successful a selection programme might be. This proportion is called the **degree of genetic determination**. If there is no genetic variation in a character in a particular population, i.e. if the degree of genetic determination is zero, then selection will have no effect on the phenotypic value of future generations. If all the variation is genetic, i.e. the degree of genetic determination is 1, then the response to selection should be rapid.

4 The degree of genetic determination is calculated as

$$\frac{V_G}{V_E + V_G}.$$

What is the degree of genetic determination of cob length in the population of maize used by East and Hayes in their experiments?

1.5 *Heritability*

Previous exercises have described how variation between individuals is due to differences both in their environments and in their genotypes. The degree of genetic determination is the proportion of the total phenotypic variation arising from genetic differences between individuals and a method for calculating it is included in exercise 1.4.

1 What is the formula for calculating the degree of genetic determination?

The genetic component of variation can be divided into two components, the **additive** and **non-additive** components. Genes are said to act **additively** when substitution of one allele for another alters the phenotypic value by a certain amount *regardless of what other alleles are present at the same or other loci*. Let us look at additive effects at a single gene locus 'A'. The phenotypic value of the heterozygote a^1a^2 is taken as the starting point. The phenotypic value of the homozygote a^1a^1 differs from the heterozygote by $-d$ and the phenotypic value of a^2a^2 differs by $+d$. The phenotypic value of the heterozygote a^1a^2 is therefore exactly at the midpoint, m (figure 1.5.1). Substituting one allele for the other in any genotype will cause a change in the phenotypic value of exactly d (either $+d$ or $-d$). Additive genetic variation is the component of the total variation which is due to many gene loci acting in this way.

Figure 1.5.1 *Additive effects at a single gene locus*

a^1a^1	a^1a^2	a^2a^2
$-d$	m	$+d$

2 As a hypothetical example, take egg weight in poultry. Let variation in egg weight be influenced by two gene loci 'A' and 'B'. Let the average egg weight of $a^1a^2 \; b^1b^2$ hens be 65 g. The value of d for the 'A' locus is 2 g and the value of d for the 'B' locus is 3 g. What would be the average weight of eggs laid by hens with the genotypes
(a) $a^1a^1 \; b^1b^2$, (b) $a^1a^2 \; b^2b^2$, (c) $a^2a^2 \; b^2b^2$?

Genes are said to act **non-additively** when the effect on the phenotype of substituting one allele for another depends on the genotype you start with and the allele which is substituted. Non-additivity due to complete dominance is illustrated in figure 1.5.2. In this figure, a^2 is completely dominant to a^1. Changing an a^2 allele to an a^1 allele in a^2a^2 has no effect on the phenotype but making the same substitution in a^1a^2 reduces the phenotypic value by 2d.

Figure 1.5.2 *Dominance effects at a single locus*

| | a^1a^2 | |
a^1a^1	a^2a^2	
$-d$	m	$+d$

The component of the total variation which is due to many genes acting in this way is called the **dominance component**. There is another component of non-additive genetic variance, called the **epistatic component**. This is due to interaction between alleles at different gene loci. The total genetic variation, V_G, in a population can be written

$$V_G = V_A + V_D + V_I$$

where

V_A is variation due to additivity,
V_D is variation due to dominance and
V_I is variation due to epistatic interaction.

Figure 1.5.3 gives a summary of these various components. The proportions shown are arbitrary and will vary among different populations.

The ratio called the degree of genetic determination describes the proportion of the phenotypic variation which is due to all three components of genetic variation. This ratio is also known as 'heritability in the broad sense'. The ratio of the additive component of genetic variance to the total phenotypic variance is usually known simply as **heritability** (or 'heritability in the narrow sense') and is given by the formula

$$\text{heritability} = \frac{V_A}{V_P}$$

Figure 1.5.3 *Summary of the components of phenotypic variation*

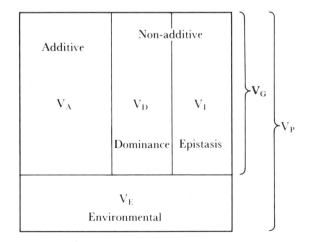

where V_A is variation due to additivity and V_P is the total phenotypic variance, $V_G + V_E$. This reflects the extent to which related individuals have similar phenotypes.

There are several methods for calculating V_A, for instance, from the results of selection experiments and from the similarities between parents and their offspring (see exercise 6.2). Any heritability estimate is, strictly speaking, applicable only to the population used in its estimation, and it is not wise to assume that other populations will give the same value because of differences between populations in the amount of genetic and environmental variation present.

3 In table 1.5.1, what do you notice about the heritabilities of characters closely associated with reproduction?

Table 1.5.1 *Approximate heritabilities for characters in domesticated animals*

Animal	Character	Approximate heritability
pig	length of legs	0.65
pig	number of vertebrae	0.74
pig	number in litter	0.15
poultry	adult body weight	0.60
poultry	egg hatchability	0.16
poultry	shell colour	0.78
cattle	milk yield	0.35
cattle	adult body weight	0.65
sheep	fleece weight	0.33
sheep	number of lambs born	0.10

4 Heritability $= \dfrac{V_A}{V_P}$

(a) If additive genetic variation is high, is heritability high or low?

(b) If environmental variation is high, is heritability high or low?

(c) What are the minimum and maximum values of heritability?

An animal or plant which leaves the most surviving offspring makes the greatest contribution to the gene pool of the next genera-

tion. In other words, natural selection will favour genes conferring greater reproductive success. For this reason there tends to be little additive genetic variation for reproductive success in a population because deleterious genes have been eliminated and favourable ones have been fixed by selection.

Estimates of heritability for any character in a particular species can vary considerably because populations will differ in the nature of their genetic variation and in the contribution of environmentally determined differences between individuals. The values given in table 1.5.1 are therefore approximate. Knowing the heritability of a character gives the breeder some idea of whether artificial selection for improvement is likely to be successful; the greater the contribution of additive genetic differences to the total variation, the greater the response to selection. Conversely, the results of a selection experiment can be used to give an estimate of the heritability of the character undergoing selection.

5 A breeder of broiler chickens has a genetically variable flock in which the mean weight at eight weeks of age is 883 g. He begins to carry out artificial selection to increase eight-week body weight by allowing only the heaviest 20% of the population to breed. The mean eight-week body weight of these birds is 997 g (figure 1.5.4). The heritability can be used to predict the expected mean eight-week body weight in the next generation. In this population the heritability of eight-week body weight is 0.6.

(a) What is the difference (in grams) between the population mean and the mean of the selected parents? This is called the **selection differential**.

(b) The difference between the mean of the starting population and the mean of all the progeny of the selected parents is called the **selection response**:

selection response =
heritability × selection differential

(i) What is the expected selection response?

Figure 1.5.4 *Variation in eight-week body weight in a flock of chickens*

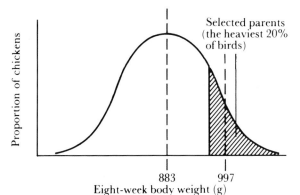

Population mean = 883 g

Mean of selected parents = 997 g

(ii) What is the expected mean eight-week body weight of the progeny of the selected parents in this experiment?

(c) Let us call the starting population S_0 and the progeny of the selected parents S_1. Your answer to (b)(ii) is the mean eight-week body weight of S_1. As before, the birds in S_1 with the heaviest eight-week body weight were selected as parents of the next generation, S_2. The selection differential in S_1 was 100 g and the selection response was 55 g.

  (i) What was the mean eight-week body weight in S_2?

 (ii) Calculate the heritability of eight-week body weight using the figures given in part (c).

(iii) Suggest a reason for the difference in heritability estimates between S_0 and S_1.

2 Selective breeding of plants and animals

Introduction

Domestication of animals probably began as far back as 10 000 BC and the cultivation of plants some two thousand years later. Right from the beginning, humans would have played a primary role in the selective forces acting on the plants and animals in close association with them. **Charles Darwin**, in his book *The Variations of Animals and Plants under Domestication*, recognised three kinds of selection acting on domesticated species: **methodical selection**, which is the deliberate modification of a population according to some predetermined standard; **unconscious selection**, which follows from neglecting the least desirable animals and plants; and **natural selection**, which acts irrespective of the domesticated state. These three kinds of selection are not mutually exclusive and are best explained by illustrations.

Methodical selection. Most modern selective breeding comes into this category which may also be described as **artificial selection**. The breeder, say of racehorses, has a clear idea of what kind of animal he or she wants and works towards producing it by mating together at each generation, animals with the most desirable characteristics.

Unconscious selection. When early farmers gathered their wheat or maize, they collected the seeds which remained attached to the plant stem and used some of this for the next season's sowing. Seeds which had fallen from brittle stems would not be collected and cultivated so there would be unconscious selection for non-brittle stems. Unconscious selection would also operate when the sheep or cattle considered least likely to survive the winter were slaughtered for meat in the preceding autumn.

Natural selection. Darwin described natural selection as a consequence of the 'struggle for existence' and later as the 'survival of the fittest' and it occurs without human interference. However, it does not cease to operate in a programme of artificial selection; for instance, a particular animal may have all the desired characteristics except that it is sterile and so cannot be used for breeding. In connection with selection and evolution, the fittest individuals are those which contribute most genes to the following generation.

The breeds of domestic animals as we know them today did not exist before the eighteenth century. In each region of the country particular types of cattle or sheep predominated but little methodical selection was practised. Any attempts to improve the local breeds had tended to concentrate on points of fashion or prejudice such as the shape of the horns. Breeding specifically for characters of economic importance was begun about the middle of the eighteenth century by **Robert Bakewell** and his contemporaries. Bakewell adopted a breeding system unusual in his day, that of pairing closely related animals, i.e. inbreeding. In sheep breeding his aim was to produce animals which most quickly repaid in meat the cost of the food they consumed. He therefore selected and bred from animals which fattened quickly, had a round barrel-shape, short legs, and small heads and bones.

Bakewell's method was one of trial and error because he had no knowledge of genetical theory. By mating together closely related animals, he produced the spectacularly successful 'New Leicester' breed of sheep but his attempts to improve Longhorn cattle by the same kind of programme was a failure. The New Longhorns put on a lot of fat, yielded less milk and were less fertile than the cattle from which he started selecting. One of the reasons for this may have been that the number of animals was too small to contain an adequate amount of genetic variation. Not only were favourable genes being lost from the breeding population but unfavourable ones were becoming homozygous. In other words the cattle showed **inbreeding depression**, a loss of fitness associated with increasing homozygosity (see exercise 1.3).

Aims and methods of selective breeding (exercises 2.1 to 2.4)

Selective breeding is practised for such purposes as to produce animals and plants adapted to marginal environments, to increase yield and quality, to reduce production costs or to improve desirable qualities in animals and plants kept for pleasure and sport.

Selection for improvement in a character involves choosing from a population certain individuals to be parents on the assumption that they carry desirable alleles which will be passed on to their offspring. Individuals which show no evidence of possessing the required alleles are not allowed to reproduce. Thus the breeder is in control of a gene pool and his or her aim is to increase the frequency of certain alleles at the expense of others. Selective breeding has been described as 'evolution at the will of man' because a person with a desired end-product in mind makes a decision about which organisms will leave offspring.

The most rapid response to selection for improvement might be expected to occur when only one or two gene loci are involved and the individuals carrying the required alleles are easily identifiable. If the character is under polygenic control and shows continuous variation, selection involves breeding from a number of individuals at the upper or lower end of the distribution of phenotypes. How far this will increase or decrease the average phenotypic value of the next generation depends on the heritability of the character.

Greater strides have been made in the selective breeding of plants than of animals for several reasons. Animals are more expensive to keep so smaller breeding units are maintained, while in plants, required phenotypes can be multiplied much more easily. When selecting parents for the next generation, the plant breeder can afford to ignore a large proportion of the population because sufficient numbers of progeny can be raised from a small number of parents. This is not so with animals. A third difficulty with the larger animals is that the generation interval is two years or more so that progress in selection is slow. The greatest advances in the breeding of animals of economic importance have been made with poultry because these have the advantages of producing relatively large numbers of offspring in a short period of time and at relatively low cost.

Species, breeds, varieties, strains and cultivars

Members of different species are **reproductively isolated** from each other, i.e. they do not normally interbreed and produce fertile progeny. Under natural conditions there is little or no gene flow between different species. However, under domestication, it is sometimes possible to cross individuals from different species to produce an **interspecific**

hybrid combining favourable features of both parental species. The mule, for example, is the offspring of a female horse which has mated with a male donkey. Mules combine the heat resistance of the donkey with the size of the horse, but they are almost always infertile. Crossing European cattle with zebu, the native cattle of India, results, however, in fully fertile progeny, proving that European and Indian cattle belong to the same species although they are quite distinct in appearance.

There is a great deal of variation between individuals within a species and by artificial selection, humans have created genetically distinct populations to suit their various requirements. In animals we call these distinct populations **breeds**. The domestic dog *Canis familiaris* with its many different breeds well illustrates the great range of variation which can be found within a species. Members of a breed share a number of distinguishing genetically determined traits but what these should be is an arbitrary decision made by people with a particular interest. A breed is a conventional rather than biological category. Animals which have the right ancestors are eligible for registration with the appropriate breed society.

In plants, genetically distinct populations are called **varieties** or cultivated varieties, shortened to **cultivars**. Within both breeds and varieties there may be subsets of individuals with special characteristics; these are called **strains**. The term **pure line** has already been introduced (exercise 1.2) and, when referring to plants, generally means that individuals are genetically identical and homozygous at all (or nearly all) gene loci. In animals a pure line is a population which is homozygous for genes controlling certain characteristics although other gene loci may be heterozygous. In both plants and animals an **inbred line** is a population where a large proportion of the gene loci are homozygous as a result of inbreeding. The extent of the homozygosity in an inbred line will vary

according to species for the reasons given in exercise 1.3.

Sources of variation (exercise 2.5)

Until less than two centuries ago, farmers raised animals and plants which were adapted to the local environment. Each area had its own characteristic varieties known as **land races**. People like Robert Bakewell and his counterparts in plant breeding used land races in crossing and inbreeding programmes to produce 'improved' varieties that became nationally and internationally popular. This trend has continued until the present day with the consequence that land races are being replaced by genetically uniform varieties. In 1946 there were seven common dairy breeds in Britain but by 1979 over 88% of all dairy cows in England and Wales belonged to the Friesian breed.

The 'green revolution' has had similar consequences for land races of cereal crops. World productivity of wheat and rice has increased dramatically since the introduction in the 1960s of high-yielding **dwarf varieties**. Farmers gave up their traditional varieties in favour of the new ones although the higher productivity of dwarf varieties is only attained under adequate levels of fertiliser treatment. It was not until after useful land races had become extinct that many farmers in third-world countries found they could not afford to buy the necessary fertilisers.

Modern dwarf cultivars of rice, now grown over vast areas, possess a single dwarfing gene derived from the Taiwanese variety Dee-geo-woo-gen. Such widespread genetic uniformity could spell disaster in the future; an example will show how. A variety of oat resistant to crown rust disease was first grown in Iowa, USA, in 1942. This variety, called Victoria, owed its resistance to a dominant gene and by 1945 the gene was present in 97% of oats grown in Iowa. The following year there was an epidemic of a different disease, oat blight, and it became apparent that plants having the dominant gene for resistance to crown rust were particularly susceptible to oat blight.

The paucity of genetic variation in some crop plants is a result of the way in which they were brought into cultivation. Millions of coffee bushes in South America are descendants of a single tree grown in Amsterdam in 1706, while the Malaysian rubber industry is based on the descendants of 22 seedlings imported from Brazil. The potatoes grown in Europe carry only a small proportion of the genes existing in Peruvian potatoes. These crops are described as having a narrow genetic base. Genetic variation is the raw material for both natural and artificial selection, and if variation is not maintained or even increased, evolution and improvement cannot occur. It is essential to compensate for the lack of genetic variation in popular breeds and varieties by maintaining populations of older animal breeds and plant varieties, together with related wild species which, although they may not be of any immediate use, act as reserves of genes for the future.

There are parts of the world rich in land races of certain plant species and their wild and weedy relatives. Such regions are known as **centres of diversity** and may be where the plants were originally cultivated. One method of conserving genetic resources would be to protect these plants in their natural environment but the uncertainties of politics and economics make this a less desirable alternative to collecting and maintaining the plants in institutions designed for that purpose. Such collections are known as **gene banks** or **germplasm collections**. The germplasm may be stored as seed or as growing plants and new methods are being developed to store plant tissues at very low temperatures.

Animal germplasm, such as embryos and bull semen, can be stored for years in liquid nitrogen but in general the preservation of animal germplasm for possible future use is limited because of the greater expense involved. Enthusiasts keep rare and/or old breeds of domestic animals for their intrinsic interest with the conservation of genetic resources being usually only a secondary consideration. Conservation of rare wild animals by maintaining breeding populations is one of the aims of modern zoos but because of limited population size, there is a real danger that these captive populations will be extinguished by inbreeding depression unless there is a conscious effort to maintain genetic variation. A good example is the cheetah in which genetic variation is very low, due, it is thought, to a population bottleneck about 10 000 years ago. Although the species has survived thus far, its numbers are on the decline.

As far as plants are concerned, new genetic variation can be induced by exposing pollen, seeds, seedlings or buds to **mutagenic chemicals** or **radiation** which bring about random changes in the DNA, as both chromosome and gene mutations. (See also exercise 2.3.) The treated plants or their progeny are then inspected to discover whether any of the induced variation is potentially valuable. In farm animals, the similar technique of irradiating males' testes or sperm to be used for artificial insemination has not been so successful in generating useful variation.

The most widely used method of introducing genetic variation into a population before or during a selection programme is to 'outcross', i.e. to mate some individuals to another variety or breed of the same species. Selection is subsequently employed to increase the frequency of the desirable genes and reduce the frequency of the undesirable ones. The required genes may be present in a different species and sometimes, especially in plants, reproductive barriers can be broken and the genes can be transferred across the species boundary. (See exercise 2.2.)

Breeding systems and selection (exercises 2.6 and 2.7)

The **breeding system** is the mode of reproduction. Some species are sexually reproducing while others are predominantly or wholly asexual. Sexually reproducing organisms may engage in inbreeding or outbreeding. The breeding system in animals of economic importance is sexual reproduction with outbreeding. Amongst cultivated plants, examples of sexual and asexual, inbreeding and outbreeding can be found. In plants and animals which are normally outbreeding, many of the gene loci in each individual are heterozygous. Enforced inbreeding in such species can lead to loss of fitness (see exercise 1.3). However, in species where inbreeding is the rule, a high proportion of the gene loci are homozygous without necessarily causing adverse effects.

Birds and mammals are incapable of self-fertilisation, the most extreme form of inbreeding, but contrary to popular belief, they have no aversion to mating with close relatives. As we have already seen, a breeding system involving inbreeding may be encouraged in some selection programmes but care must be taken to maintain fitness in the selected lines.

Like animals, dioecious plants must of necessity cross-fertilise and among hermaphrodite plants there are many adaptations to encourage cross- rather than self-pollination. Some plants have a genetically determined self-incompatibility system which ensures that only genetically unrelated pollen fertilises the ovules. The fact that such adaptations have evolved clearly demonstrates the value of outbreeding. Outbreeding maintains genetic variation in a population and so allows evolution to occur should the environment change. But variation is not maintained in order to provide an insurance policy for the future. Natural selection is opportunistic, i.e. the phenotypes which leave the most offspring are those which are best adapted to the present environment. Outbreeding may be favoured by selection because the offspring resulting from such a breeding system have a higher level of heterozygosity which contributes to a greater reproductive capacity (fitness).

It is important to know the breeding system of a species because different methods of selection are appropriate to inbreeders and outbreeders. With naturally inbreeding plants such as wheat and barley the breeder's goal is a pure line so that all the plants will be of the same quality. Farmers value uniformity of the phenotype as well as high quality and productivity but, as we have seen, inbreeding to achieve genetic uniformity is often accompanied by inbreeding depression.

Hybrid vigour (exercise 2.8)

Inbreeding depression is commonly observed as a consequence of increasing homozygosity in a normally outbreeding species. If two different inbred lines are crossed, the resulting 'hybrid' generation is genetically uniform but heterozygous at all the gene loci at which the two parental lines are homozygous for different alleles. This increase in heterozygosity sometimes results in superiority over both parental types in characters associated with reproductive fitness, e.g. lifespan, fertility, fecundity (number of offspring produced), size and resistance to disease. In other words, the hybrid offspring do not show the inbreeding depression of the parents while retaining genetic and phenotypic uniformity. Superiority of the hybrids is called **hybrid vigour** or **heterosis**. It is not only outbreeding species that can show hybrid vigour; it may be observed also in inbreeding species, such as rice.

According to one theory of heterosis, the hybrid combines favourable dominant alleles from both parents. During inbreeding, different lines become homozygous for deleterious recessive alleles at many different gene loci. Suppose one inbred line has the genotype *aa BB cc DD* and another has the genotype *AA bb CC dd*. On crossing, the hybrid will be *Aa Bb Cc Dd* and so is homozygous for none of the alleles. No single theory can account for heterosis and it seems very likely that epistatic interaction and linkage play some part.

Heterozygosity in itself may be important because if both alleles at a locus each give rise to a functional gene product the heterozygous organism may be more versatile in its metabolic processes.

Exercise 2.8 illustrates how hybrid vigour is exploited in maize where inbred lines, although low yielding, are maintained because they produce exceptionally good hybrids on crossing. In pig farming, the premium is on fecundity; the farmer wants from each sow as many piglets as possible. Commercial pig-breeders maintain pure breeds which are then mated to each other (cross-bred) to produce F_1 hybrids. The farmer buys the F_1 sows in the expectation that they will show hybrid vigour in fecundity. The same system operates in intensive egg production where the laying hens are almost always hybrids between selected lines.

Polyploidy (exercise 2.9)

Interspecific (between species) hybrids such as the mule may combine favourable features of both parental species, a phenomenon which is sometimes loosely described as 'hybrid vigour'. Interspecific hybrids are usually sterile because their two sets of chromosomes, one from each parental species, are not homologous so cannot pair in prophase of meiosis, with the result that no gametes are formed. Natural interspecific hybridisation is fairly common amongst plants and occasionally the hybrid undergoes a doubling of all its chromosomes. Doubling means that each chromosome gains a homologue and meiosis and gamete formation can proceed normally.

A hybrid which has undergone chromosome doubling has four sets of chromosomes instead of two. Organisms which have more than two sets of chromosomes, are called **polyploids** and if their chromosomes have come from different species they are called **allopolyploids**. Exercise 2.9 shows how allopolyploidy has played a part in the evolution of several crop plants. Although polyploidy is widespread in the plant kingdom, it is rare in animals, probably because the normal method of sex determination is disrupted by chromosome doubling.

Summary and conclusion

In the absence of genetic variation progress cannot be made in either natural or artificial selection. Most breeds of domesticated animals and plant cultivars contain only a small proportion of the total genetic variation present in the species so one method of introducing new genes into a population is to outcross to another variety of the same species. If utilisable genetic variation does not exist then it may be possible to generate it by employing mutagenic agents. Alternatively, genes from other species may be introduced by interspecific crosses. In the evolution of plants, novel variation has arisen by interspecific hybridisation combining chromosomes from different sources and we have succeeded in copying this natural phenomenon. In chapter 5 we shall see how new techniques of gene manipulation promise to make significant contributions to plant and animal breeding.

2.1 Selection in sweet peas

The sweet pea is a popular garden flower which was first grown in Britain in 1699. Like the garden pea, it is a naturally self-pollinating species and a number of different varieties have arisen spontaneously. Before 1900, all varieties had medium-sized flowers with plain standards but in the years 1900, 1901 and 1902 a mutant form occurred in the variety Prima Donna in four separate localities. This new form had larger flowers and a waved standard and was named Countess Spencer.

1 When Countess Spencer sweet peas were allowed to self-fertilise, all the progeny were of the Countess Spencer type. What does this suggest about the difference in

genotype between Countess Spencer and Prima Donna?

2 How can you explain the fact that the new form arose in four different localities within a space of two years?

Prima Donna is pink but today the large-flowered type with waved standards is available in many different colours. When Countess Spencer (pink, with waved standards) is crossed with the variety King Edward (red, with plain standards) the progeny are all red and the F_2 plants appear in the ratio 3 red : 1 pink.

3 A breeder has the varieties Countess Spencer and King Edward. Explain in detail the practical procedure he must carry out in order to produce a pure breeding red variety with waved standards.

2.2 *Breeding tomatoes for resistance to eelworm*

Wide crosses are crosses between different species and are often used in plant breeding to transfer resistance to pests and diseases from wild into cultivated species. The cultivated tomato *Lycopersicon esculentum* is susceptible to potato cyst-eelworm, a widespread and persistent pest of tomatoes and potatoes in the UK. *Lycopersicon pimpinellifolium* is a wild species of tomato and easily hybridises with the cultivated species. The fruits of the wild species are of poor quality but the plants are resistant to potato cyst-eelworm.

When *L. esculentum* variety 'Ailsa Craig' was crossed to *L. pimpinellifolium*, all the F_1 hybrids were resistant. The F_2 generation derived from selfing the F_1 plants showed a ratio of 3 resistant : 1 susceptible, suggesting that resistance was caused by a dominant allele at a single gene locus. The F_1 and F_2 plants showed a reduction in yield and quality of fruits because half the genes in each generation were

derived from the wild *L. pimpinellifolium* parent.

The gene for resistance was transferred into the cultivated tomato by a system of back-crossing and subsequent selection of the resistant progeny. The F_1 hybrids were back-crossed to *L. esculentum* and the resulting generation was called BC-1. BC-2 was obtained by crossing the resistant plants in BC-1 to *L. esculentum*. The same procedure was carried out for six generations, to BC-6.

1 What percentage of plants in the BC-1 generation would be resistant to eelworm?

2 The F_1 generation was obtained by crossing *L. esculentum* with *L. pimpinellifolium* so half of the total number of genes in the F_1 generation came from each species. When the F_1 plants are backcrossed to *L. esculentum*, what percentage of all the genes in the BC-1 generation originate from *L. esculentum*?

3 As the backcrossing of resistant progeny continues each generation, the percentage of *L. esculentum* genes increases. What will be the proportion of *L. esculentum* genes in (a) BC-2, (b) BC-4. (c) BC-6?

The yield and quality of fruit in the sixth backcross generation was found to be comparable to the original Ailsa Craig variety, but the genotype was not yet suitable for release on to the market as a resistant cultivar because the resistant BC-6 plants were not pure breeding.

4 (a) If the resistant BC-6 plants were allowed to self-fertilise, what would be the ratio of resistant to non-resistant plants in their offspring?
   (b) What proportion of the resistant offspring would be pure breeding?
   (c) How could these plants be identified?

5 Assume a generation interval of one year. How many years will it have taken to produce a variety of *L. esculentum* pure breeding for resistance to potato cyst-eelworm?

2.3 Autosexing poultry and silkworms

The breeding of chickens suitable for battery conditions is carried out by large firms. Battery chickens are hybrids between strains selected for egg production, food conversion efficiency and disease resistance. The strains used for crossing are chosen for their ability to give progeny showing hybrid vigour.

The birds are sold as day-old chicks and egg producers want to purchase only females. It is skilled and time-consuming work to sex newly hatched chicks by examination of the genitalia and in the 1930s there was some interest in the production of 'autosexing' breeds, where males and females could be identified by their plumage. Such breeds were never popular because they were less productive than highly selected and hybrid birds, but they provide an interesting example of the application of simple Mendelian principles to commercial breeding.

The Barred Plymouth Rock has black feathers with a white bar across each one. The barring is due to an X-linked allele B. In birds, females are the heterogametic sex (XY) and males are homogametic (XX). Plymouth Rock males are therefore homozygous for the B allele while females are hemizygous (i.e. have just one B allele, on the X chromosome). In the light feathered Golden Campine breed, the allele for barring is normally absent but when it is introduced, by repeated backcrossing (see exercise 2.2), homozygous male chicks are paler in colour than hemizygous females. By transfer of the B allele from Barred Plymouth Rock into Golden Campine, a new autosexing breed called 'Cambar' was created.

1 If Golden Campine females (X^bY) are mated to Barred Plymouth Rock males, what will be the genotypes of the F_1 males and females?

2 If these progeny are crossed amongst themselves, what will be the genotypes of the F_2 males and females?

The silkworm is another species in which it is essential to be able to recognise males and females at an early age. The silkworm is the caterpillar of a moth, *Bombyx mori*, and at this stage it is difficult to identify the sex although it is desirable to do so before emergence of the adults for two reasons. First, it is necessary to prevent matings between members of the same strain because crosses are made between two different selected strains in order to exploit hybrid vigour in silk production. Second, male silkworms are economically more important than females as they are more efficient in converting mulberry leaves, their food plant, into silk.

Sex determination in moths is the same as in birds, with the female the heterogametic sex, XY. In the silkworm, there are no convenient sex-linked genes which allow easy identification of the sexes at an early age but there are several gene loci on the autosomes at which there are mutant alleles affecting egg colour. One of these is w on chromosome 10. Homozygous ww eggs are yellow instead of the dark brown of eggs carrying the dominant allele W. By exposing heterozygous female pupae to X-rays, Japanese geneticists were able to induce a translocation between the Y-chromosome and the desired part of the 10th chromosome. In other words, a suitable marker gene was transferred to a sex chromosome. Although X-ray treatment brings about mutation, it cannot be directed to produce only those required. The progeny of treated individuals must be inspected to discover whether they carry useful radiation-induced variation. In the silkworm this was done by mating irradiated heterozygous Ww females with homozygous ww males.

3 (a) The 'W' locus is on a pair of autosomes (chromosome 10). If irradiation had no effect at all on its inheritance, what would be the colours of the eggs produced by these heterozygous females and in what proportions would they occur?

(b) Would XY (female) and XX (male) eggs be distinguishable by their colour?

Further crossing led to the discovery of a female in which the dominant *W* allele had been translocated to the Y chromosome. A female egg which carries this translocation as well as being homozygous *ww* at the normal locus on chromosome 10, is dark brown. Such females, i.e. $XY^W ww$, were used to establish an autosexing strain. Many such strains are now used in commercial silk production.

4 (a) Using the gene symbols given above, show the genotype of the males in the autosexing strain.

(b) By means of a Punnett square or similar diagram, show the genotypes and phenotypes of the eggs produced by the autosexing strain.

5 Compare the genetic basis of autosexing in 'Cambar' poultry and silkworms.

2.4 Breeding cattle for milk

Eighteenth-century cattle breeders, although ignorant of genetical theory, were able to make improvements in the yield and quality of beef and milk in their herds by breeding from the most desirable animals. An understanding of the genetical basis of these continuous characters has made it possible to increase the rate of improvement and to avoid making expensive mistakes.

1 Figure 2.4.1 shows the percentage of butterfat (cream) in the milk of two breeds of cattle, their F_1 hybrids and two backcrosses. The backcross progeny were obtained by crossing F_1 animals to either Red Dane or Jersey.

(a) What evidence is there that butterfat percentage is a heritable character?

(b) What are the possible causes of variation in butterfat percentage within the Jersey herd?

2 On the basis of the information given in figure 2.4.1, do you think that mean butterfat percentage could be improved by selection of the highest scoring animals in

(a) the Jersey herd, and

(b) the F_1 hybrid herd?

Give reasons for your answers.

3 Consider the graphs in figure 2.4.2 (page 24) and suggest reasons

(a) for the low milk yield in 1918–19 and 1941–44;

(b) why butterfat percentage was not affected in 1918–19 and 1941–44;

(c) for the increase in percentage butterfat between 1905 and 1945.

In the past the main method of improving milk yields was to compare cows in the same herd and to breed from those with the highest yield. Comparison of animals kept under the same environmental conditions is called **performance testing**. A cow can give birth to a maximum of only about eight calves in a lifetime and on average only half of these will be female, but the method of **embryo transfer** is now available to increase the reproductive capacity of particularly desirable cows. By hormone treatment, a cow can be induced to superovulate, i.e. release several ova at once. If these are all fertilised, up to twelve embryos may begin to develop in the uterus at the same time. Within a few days of fertilisation, the embryos are washed out of the uterus and each can be transferred directly into another cow or deep frozen for later implantation. In this state, the embryos and the genes they carry can be transported easily, even across the world.

Performance testing is applicable only to characters which can be measured in the potential parents such as conformation (shape) or growth rate in beef cattle. For female characters like milk production, there is no way of telling from a bull's phenotype whether he carries desirable genes. The way to find out is to allow him to breed with several

Figure 2.4.1 *Percentage butterfat in Red Dane, Jersey, their F$_1$ hybrids and backcrosses*

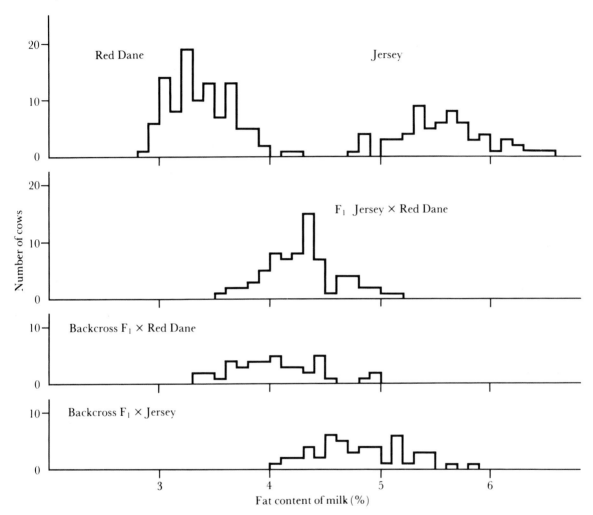

cows and then compare the average performance of a number of his daughters with the progeny of other males. This is called **progeny testing**.

If the results of the progeny test are satisfactory, that bull can be used to sire (father) more offspring. By natural mating a bull can pass on his genes to many more offspring than can a cow and by **artificial insemination (AI)** his progeny can number as many as 10 000 per year. Because of the time taken for first the bull and then his daughters to reach maturity, he cannot be progeny tested until he is about five years old, leaving about another five or six years of serviceable life. However, now that it can be kept deep frozen for long periods, the semen from a good bull can be used for many years after the death of the donor.

4 Why is it important in both performance testing and progeny testing that the animals to be compared are maintained in a similar environment?

Figure 2.4.2 *Average butterfat percentage and yield of milk of Danish cows from 1904 to 1944*

5 Milk yield is a very complex character and one factor which determines whether a cow produces any milk at all is whether she is fertile. Why is fertility an important factor in milk production?

A consequence of the use of AI is that the better sires can be used to fertilise more cows, with the result that milk yield per cow will be increased in future generations. On the other hand, if fewer bulls are used as sires there may be a decline in the genetic variation within the breed and an increase in inbreeding depression.

6 A newly arisen mutant allele results in foot deformities when homozygous but has no effect when heterozygous. A particular bull is heterozygous for this new mutant allele.
 (a) If the bull's semen is used to fertilise several thousand cows, which produce a total of 4000 daughters, how many daughters are expected to carry this deleterious recessive allele?
 (b) If the same semen is used to fertilise a random sample of these 4000 daughters, what proportion of the offspring are expected to be homozygous for this allele?

2.5 *The search for better soybeans*

The soybean (*Glycine max*) is a traditional crop in China and is now grown in other parts of the world for both human and animal consumption. The beans are rich in protein and are used in the manufacture of meat substitutes. However, the raw beans contain proteins which inhibit the growth of animals, including one known as the Kunitz trypsin inhibitor, and so before consumption the beans must be heated to destroy these proteins.

1 What would be the effect of a high temperature on a globular protein such as trypsin inhibitor?

2 What is trypsin and where is it produced in a mammal?

3 How could inhibition of trypsin activity account for inhibition of growth?

Orf and Hymowitz searched through the germplasm collection of soybeans in the USA, looking for a variety which did not contain trypsin inhibitor. To do this it was necessary to separate the proteins present in each bean by a technique called **electrophoresis**.

Electrophoresis separates molecules from a mixture according to their charge and size. A sample of the mixture is placed in a slot in a medium such as a starch or polyacrylamide gel which is at a certain pH (figure 2.5.1(a)). The pH of the sample and gel are carefully

Figure 2.5.1 *The technique of electrophoresis*

(a) Running the gel

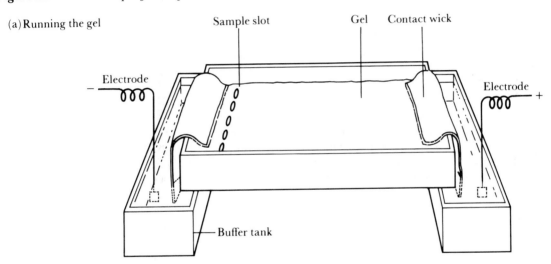

(b) Staining the gel

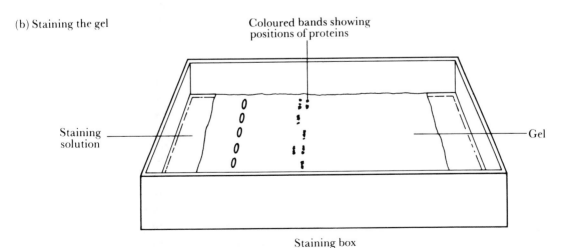

controlled using buffer solutions because the charges on the molecules to be separated are affected by the pH of the surrounding medium. An electric current is then passed through the gel and positively charged ions (cations) in the sample migrate to the cathode while negatively charged ions (anions) migrate to the anode. Normally the pH is adjusted so that the ions of interest are all negatively charged. The sample can then be placed near the cathode end of the gel giving a longer run to the anode and therefore better separation.

The electric current is the motive force, pulling the charged proteins from the sample slot towards the appropriate electrode. The greater the charge on the particle, the faster it would be expected to move but the gel acts like a kind of sieve, letting smaller molecules migrate faster than larger ones. The result is that after an hour or more the proteins are distributed through the gel. To make them visible they must be stained (figure 2.5.1(b)).

In their survey of three thousand soybean varieties, Orf and Hymowitz found three kinds of trypsin inhibitor (abbreviated to SBTI). The results of electrophoresis of beans from three different plants are shown in figure 2.5.2.

SBTI is a protein and is encoded in DNA. Two hypotheses can be proposed to account for the existence of three different SBTIs.

Hypothesis 1 There is one gene locus with three alleles, each one coding for a different SBTI.

Hypothesis 2 The three SBTIs are coded for by three different gene loci.

4 Which of the two hypotheses above is supported by the following information? Explain your answer.
  (i) Soybean is self-fertilising and it can be assumed that all the varieties were homozygous at the locus or loci for SBTI.
  (ii) None of the varieties screened had more than one kind of SBTI.
  (iii) Alleles which produce no SBTI are very rare.

Crosses were made between plants which had different SBTIs. Seeds were first analysed to find out which SBTI they produced by carrying out electrophoresis on a portion of the seed opposite the embryo. The rest of the seed was allowed to germinate and, at flowering, the required crosses were made. Figure 2.5.3 shows the electrophoresis patterns of the parent plants and their F_1 progeny.

5 Assume there is a single gene locus which codes for SBTI.
  (a) Why are there two SBTI bands in the electrophoresis pattern of the F_1 progeny?
  (b) If the type A × type C F_1 progeny were allowed to self-fertilise, what would be the electrophoresis patterns of the F_2 progeny and in what ratio would they be expected?

Orf and Hymowitz deduced from their results that a single gene locus was responsible for the production of SBTI. They called the three alleles which produced the different SBTIs Ti^a, Ti^b and Ti^c. They also discovered a fourth allele, ti, which produced no detectable SBTI. This potentially useful allele occurred in only two varieties, both collected in Korea, in the whole germplasm collection.

Figure 2.5.2 *Relative distances travelled by three kinds of trypsin inhibitors*

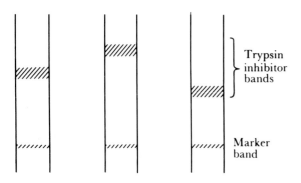

Trypsin inhibitor bands

Marker band

Figure 2.5.3 *Electrophoresis patterns of three pairs of parent plants and their progeny*

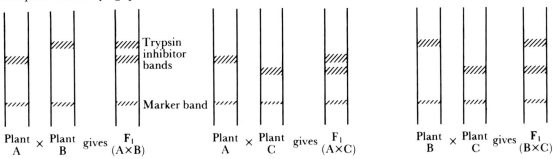

6 A plant with the genotype $Ti^a Ti^a$ is crossed to one with the genotype *ti ti*. Describe the SBTI electrophoresis pattern of both parents and the F_1 beans.

7 A plant with the genotype $Ti^a Ti^b$ is crossed to another with the genotype $Ti^a Ti^c$ as shown in figure 2.5.4.

   (a) Using similar diagrams, show the electrophoresis patterns of their progeny and give their genotypes.
   (b) In what proportions would these genotypes be expected?

This exercise has illustrated the power of the technique of electrophoresis in allowing us to see the gene products directly and therefore to determine genotypes without having to carry out test crosses. Its application in the 1960s to wild populations of animals and plants

Figure 2.5.4 *Electrophoresis patterns of parents in the cross $Ti^a Ti^b$ × $Ti^a Ti^c$*

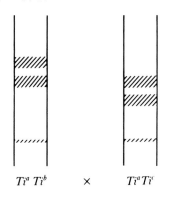

revealed a previously unsuspected amount of protein polymorphism, reflecting genetic variation. The same technique coupled with the use of enzymes which cut DNA is now allowing us to see variation in the genetic material itself (see DNA fingerprinting, chapter 6).

2.6 Breeding systems

All animals of commercial importance are sexually reproducing and the sexes are separate but the habitual mode of reproduction or **breeding system** in plants varies with the species. Plants important in agriculture fall into two main groups, the mainly self-fertilising species and the mainly cross-fertilising species. Some examples are given in table 2.6.1.

A breeding system involving continued self-fertilisation results in a high level of homozygosity (exercise 1.3) and with naturally self-fertilising plants, the aim of the breeder is usually to produce a variety which is homozygous for the desired alleles and therefore pure breeding for the required phenotype. In contrast, individual plants in naturally cross-fertilising species are heterozygous at a large proportion of their gene loci. This heterozygosity contributes to their fitness (exercise 2.7) and must be maintained during the breeding programme or restored at the end of it (exercise 2.8).

Table 2.6.1 *Breeding systems of some crop plants*

Self-fertilising

Apricot	Peanut
Aubergine	Rice
Barley	Soybean
Lettuce	Tobacco
Pea	Tomato
Peach	Wheat

Cross-fertilising

Apple	Maize
*Asparagus	Onion
Brussels sprouts	Pear
Cabbage	Plum
*Date	Runner bean
Fig	*Spinach

*dioecious

A third system of reproduction is by asexual means and this can be exploited by the plant breeder in that desirable genotypes produced by genetic recombination can be perpetuated by vegetative propagation. Asexually produced offspring are genetically identical to the parent, to each other and to all their own progeny. A population of such organisms, all derived asexually from a single parent, is called a **clone**. Agriculturally important plants which are clonally propagated include fruit and nut trees, roses, pineapples, bananas, sugar cane, potato, sweet potato, strawberry, blackberry and raspberry.

1 Distinguish between sexual and asexual reproduction. In your answer, use the words meiosis, mitosis, gametes and fertilisation.

2 Consider the statements A–F below.
   A A single parent plant is sufficient.
   B Heterozygous plants *Aa* can produce homozygous *AA* or *aa* offspring.
   C Homozygous *AA* or *aa* plants can produce heterozygous *Aa* offspring.
   D Plants with the genotype *AA bb* or *aa BB* can produce in future generations and

without mutation, plants with the genotype *aa bb* or *AA BB*.
   E Gene combinations in the parent are not disrupted by recombination.
   F The method of reproduction allows a high level of heterozygosity in the population.
State whether each of the statements above is true of
   (i) asexual reproduction;
   (ii) sexual reproduction by self-fertilisation;
   (iii) sexual reproduction by cross-fertilisation.

3 Explain how each of the statements A–F above illustrates a possible advantage for the survival of the species.

4 Discuss whether each of the following is or is not an adaptation favouring cross-fertilisation rather than self-fertilisation.
   (a) The plants are dioecious (male and female flowers on separate plants).
   (b) The plants are monoecious (separate male and female flowers on the same plant).
   (c) The flowers are hermaphrodite (functional anthers and ovules in the same flower).
   (d) The flowers are protandrous (anthers release pollen before stigmas of the same flower are receptive).
   (e) The pollen grains are smooth and light.
   (f) The pollen grains are short lived.

Self-fertilisation leads to an increase in the level of homozygosity, thus reducing genetic variation and adaptability to a changing environment, but there are advantages in the short term. Natural selection favouring a change in the breeding system from outcrossing (cross-fertilisation) to self-fertilisation has occurred in many plant genera, a familiar example being the garden pea, *Pisum sativum*. The pea is normally self-fertilising and highly homozygous, making it a suitable subject for the study of inheritance, and yet the pea flower shows structural adaptations for cross-pollination by insects. The same is true of other cultivated legumes such as peanut, mung bean, french bean, chick pea and soya bean but the runner bean is an outcrossing species and a good harvest depends on the availability of insect pollinators.

2.7 Self-incompatibility in plants

Many plants show adaptations to encourage cross-pollination but this does not necessarily insure against inbreeding. Seeds and pollen are normally dispersed within a limited area meaning that neighbouring plants, which are most likely to fertilise each other, are often also closely related to each other.

In many species there exists a means of recognition between genetically related plants. If pollen lands on a stigma with a similar genotype, the pollen tube fails to reach an ovule and so fertilisation does not occur. This mechanism is called **self-incompatibility** and is usually controlled by a single gene locus known as 'S' at which there are many different alleles, s_1, s_2, s_3, s_4 etc.; the forage

legume *Trifolium pratense* (red clover) is known to have at least 212 alleles at this locus. All diploid cells of a plant, including stigmas, possess any two of these alleles and haploid pollen grain nuclei possess one. In the **gametophytic** self-incompatibility system, the genotype of the pollen grain itself (the gametophyte) determines its reaction with a stigma.

1 If the stigma of a flower has the genotype s_1s_2, what are the genotypes of the pollen grains in the same flower?

If a pollen grain lands on a stigma possessing the same allele as itself it is not able to fertilise an egg cell because the pollen tube does not grow (figure 2.7.1). Not only does this lead to self-incompatibility but also to incompatibility between any pollen and stigmas carrying the same allele.

2 Table 2.7.1 shows possible pairings between plants with five different genotypes. A minus sign indicates that no fertilisation at all will result from that pairing. In all the other pairings, either half or all of the pollen is capable of fertilising the egg cells.

Figure 2.7.1 *Gametophytic self-incompatibility*

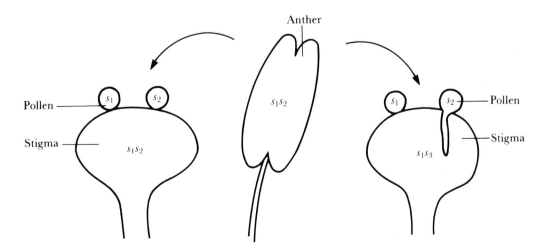

Table 2.7.1   *Consequences of gametophytic self-incompatibility*

Genotype of pollen parent	Genotype of stigma				
	s_1s_2	s_1s_3	s_2s_3	s_2s_4	s_3s_4
s_1s_2	–				
s_1s_3		–			
s_2s_3			–		
s_2s_4				–	
s_3s_4					–

Copy table 2.7.1 and write in the appropriate boxes 'all' or '$\frac{1}{2}$' where all or only half the pollen can bring about fertilisation.

3 What are the possible genotypes of the zygotes in the following crosses?

    Male plant   Female plant
(a) s_1s_2 × s_1s_3
(b) s_1s_3 × s_2s_3
(c) s_1s_2 × s_3s_4

4 In the gametophytic self-incompatibility system just described, is it possible for a plant to be homozygous for any one 'S' allele? Explain your answer.

Among cultivated plants, apples, pears, plums and cherries have gametophytic self-incompatibility systems, Victoria plums being one of the few self-compatible varieties. For the majority, it is necessary to grow in the same orchard two different varieties which flower simultaneously and can fertilise each other, otherwise no fruit will be set. Care must be taken in choosing appropriate varieties because some, such as the pears Laxton's Superb and Williams' Bon Chrétien, have the same incompatibility alleles.

5 Suggest why apple, pear, plum and cherry trees are almost always propagated asexually by grafting rather than by seed.

Another type of incompatibility system is called **sporophytic** because the incompatibility phenotype of the pollen grain is determined by the genotype of the parent plant (the sporophyte) which produces the pollen. This system is also controlled by a locus called 'S' but it is possible for one allele to be dominant. Let s_1 be dominant to s_2. The dominance effect operates on the pollen while it is forming so *all* pollen produced by s_1s_2 plants has the s_1 phenotype regardless of its own genotype. The female tissue behaves in the same way as in the gametophytic system. Thus s_2 pollen produced by an s_1s_2 plant will not grow on any stigma which contains s_1 (figure 2.7.2).

Figure 2.7.2 *Sporophytic self-incompatibility, where s_1 is dominant to s_2*

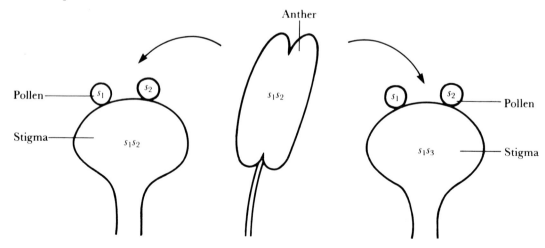

6 (a) Copy table 2.7.2, making the boxes 2 cm square.
   (b) Assume that S_1 is dominant to all other alleles. Insert minus signs where there will be no fertilisation.
   (c) Where fertilisation can occur, write in the possible genotypes of the zygotes.

Table 2.7.2 *Consequences of sporophytic self-incompatibility*

Genotype of pollen parent	Genotype of stigma		
	S_1S_2	S_1S_3	S_2S_3
S_1S_2			
S_1S_3			

7 Is it possible for a plant to be homozygous for an 'S' allele if incompatibility is of the sporophytic type?

Sporophytic self-incompatibility is found in *Brassica oleracea*, a tremendously variable species which includes cauliflowers, broccoli, cabbages and Brussels sprouts. Exercise 2.8 illustrates how, in maize, controlled crossing between certain varieties is carried out for the purpose of producing hybrid seed. In *Brassica*, the stamens and stigmas are close together in small flowers so it is impossible to make large-scale controlled crosses by removing stamens. However, exploitation of the sporophytic self-incompatibility system has allowed the development of genetically uniform F_1 hybrid varieties of Brussels sprouts and other *Brassicas*.

2.8 Hybrid corn

One of the most significant applications of genetics to agriculture is the exploitation of hybrid vigour in the species where it was first discovered, corn or maize, *Zea mays*.

Maize is a member of the grass family and bears separate male and female flowers. The male inflorescence occurs at the top of the plant and is called the tassel while the female inflorescences are borne laterally and, after fertilisation, develop into the familiar 'corn on the cob'.

Hybrid seed corn sold to farmers is produced by cross-fertilisation. It is therefore essential that the 'tassels' containing the anthers are removed from the plants which are to produce the seed ('female' plants) so that self-fertilisation cannot occur. Rows of de-tasselled plants and rows of intact plants are grown together in the same field. The intact plants belong to a different inbred line and provide pollen for fertilisation of the female plants.

1 De-tasselled 'female' plants (inbred line A) with the genotype *GG hh JJ kk* are grown together with intact pollen-producing plants (inbred line B) with the genotype *gg HH jj KK*. What will be the genotype of the embryos in the cobs borne on (a) line A, (b) line B?

Hybrid seeds are collected from line A but the parent plants have a low yield because they are inbred. A refinement of the technique utilises 'double crosses' and is illustrated in figure 2.8.1. The (A×B) female parent is itself a hybrid so produces more seed.

Figure 2.8.1 *Production of hybrid seed using the double cross method*

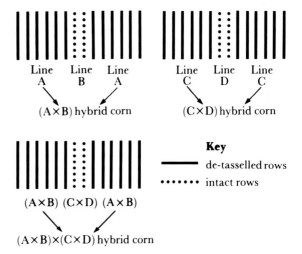

Line A   Line B   Line A
(A×B) hybrid corn

Line C   Line D   Line C
(C×D) hybrid corn

(A×B) (C×D) (A×B)
(A×B)×(C×D) hybrid corn

Key
—— de-tasselled rows
······ intact rows

2 If line C has the genotype *GG HH jj kk* and line D has the genotype *gg hh JJ KK*, what is the genotype of (C×D) plants?

3 How many different genotypes are possible (for the four gene loci 'G', 'H', 'I' and 'J') in the progeny of (A×B) × (C×D)?

These hybrid progeny are not so uniform as those resulting from a single cross (e.g. A×B or C×D) but this disadvantage is outweighed by the higher yield of seed by the hybrid female plants. There remains sufficient heterozygosity in the progeny of double crosses to give superior yields. However, the majority of hybrid corn is again produced by the single cross technique because it has been possible to produce by selection inbred lines which are capable of high seed production.

   Whether single or double crosses are used, the 'female' plants must be de-tasselled by hand or machine before the pollen is shed. This is a laborious and expensive procedure and mutant plants were sought which failed to make viable pollen. Eventually such a plant was found in Texas. Something in the cytoplasm (a mitochondrial gene) prevented the formation of pollen so making the plant 'male sterile'. The next stage was to transfer the Texas cytoplasm into the desired inbred lines. A plant receives all its cytoplasm (and mitochondria) from the female parent.

4 Figure 2.8.2 represents the nucleus and cytoplasm of the Texas male sterile plant, of a male fertile inbred line and the required combination. Explain the breeding procedure that would have to be used in order to obtain the required combination.

The production of hybrid corn involves the same kind of planting pattern as with hand de-tasselled plants, that is, growing rows of male sterile plants with rows of male fertile plants in between as pollinators (see figure 2.8.1). The hybrid seed is collected from the male sterile plants.

Figure 2.8.2 *Diagrammatic representation of the nucleus and cytoplasm of Texas male sterile (T), a male fertile inbred line (i) and the required combination*

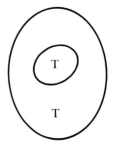

Texas male sterile

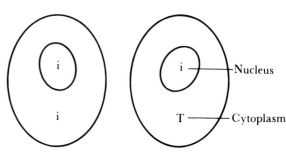

Inbred male fertile   Required combination
                        (Texas cytoplasm with
                        chromosomes from
                        inbred line)

5 If a farmer bought this seed, what planting pattern would he have to use in order to ensure that his cytoplasmic male sterile hybrid corn would be fertilised?

Ideally, a farmer should be able to sow hybrid seed which is self-fertile. This is possible due to the discovery in a different variety of corn of a dominant fertility restorer gene (*Rf*) which is found in the nucleus and counteracts the effects of male sterile cytoplasm. Male sterile plants have the genotype *rf/rf*.

6 The hybrid seed which the farmer receives is represented in figure 2.8.3. Using similar diagrams, show the genotype and cytoplasm type of the male (pollinator) and female parents involved in its production. The female parent is male sterile.

Figure 2.8.3 *One cell of the embryo of a hybrid seed containing chromosomal Rf gene and cytoplasmic sterility factor*

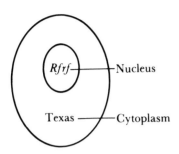

An epidemic disease of oats in 1946 had demonstrated one of the hazards of genetic uniformity but this warning went unheeded. In 1970 it was discovered that corn with Texas cytoplasm was highly susceptible to the disease called southern corn leaf blight. By this time 85% of hybrid corn contained Texas cytoplasm and there ensued one of the most severe epidemics ever known. Since then, the use of Texas cytoplasm has declined and de-tasselling by hand is again employed in the production of hybrid corn.

2.9 Polyploidy in crop plant evolution

Polyploid organisms are those which have more than two sets of chromosomes in their somatic cells. The kind of polyploids most important in crop plant evolution are those where the sets of chromosomes have come from different species and so are called **allopolyploids** ('allo' means 'other'). A basic set consists of a certain number of chromosomes called the **monoploid** number and is referred to as 'x'. Most animals have in their somatic cells two representatives of each chromosome, i.e. they are **diploid** ($2x$). The word **haploid** will be more familiar to you than monoploid. The haploid number is the number of chromosomes present in the gametes but this is not always the same as the monoploid number, as we shall see. The haploid number is referred to as 'n' and the number of chromosomes in somatic cells is called $2n$. In diploids therefore, $2n = 2x$. Plants are commonly polyploid, having three (**triploid**), four (**tetraploid**) or even more sets of chromosomes. In a tetraploid plant the chromosome number in somatic cells ($2n$) is $4x$ and the number in the gametes (n) is $2x$.

Polyploids are of value for three reasons. They tend to have larger cells and this is often reflected in the generally larger size of the plant, e.g. the cultivated strawberry is octoploid ($8x$). Polyploids with uneven numbers of chromosome sets ($3x$, $5x$ etc.) are sterile and may be useful for the production of seedless fruits such as watermelons. Probably the greatest value of allopolyploidy lies in extending the range of adaptation of the plant as a result of the combination of characteristics from two species.

Natural allopolyploids are not uncommon in cultivated species and the evolution of bread wheat provides a good example (figure 2.9.1).

Natural allopolyploidy seems to have come about in several ways.

A Haploid gametes from both parental species fuse to form a fertile hybrid.

B Haploid gametes from both species fuse to form a sterile diploid hybrid which then undergoes chromosome doubling, resulting in a fertile tetraploid.

C A haploid gamete from one diploid species fuses with an unreduced (diploid) gamete from the other species. The resulting triploid is sterile but may undergo chromosome doubling which restores fertility.

D One or both of the parental species may be polyploid. A normal gamete from one species fuses with an unreduced gamete from the other. The resulting polyploid may or may not be fertile.

Figure 2.9.1   *Scheme showing the evolution of bread wheat by allopolyploidy*

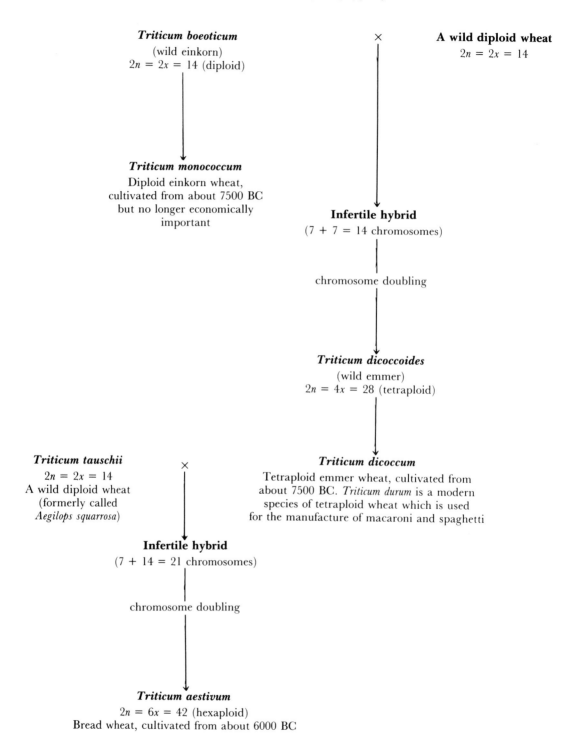

1 Explain how each of the following allopolyploid species (in bold type) may have arisen from the parental species. (The exact parental species are not always known. Where the polyploidy is very ancient, as in cotton, the true parental species may no longer exist.)

(a) *Gossypium herbaceum* × *G. raimondii*
$2n = 2x = 26$ ↓ $2n = 2x = 26$
G. hirsutum (cotton)
$2n = 4x = 52$

(b) *Musa acuminata* × *M. balbisiana*
$2n = 2x = 22$ ↓ $2n = 2x = 22$
Edible banana
$3x = 33$

(c) *Nicotiana sylvestris* × *N. tomentosiformis*
$2n = 2x = 24$ ↓ $2n = 2x = 24$
N. tabacum (tobacco)
$2n = 4x = 48$

(d) *Fragaria virginiana* × *F. chiloensis*
$2n = 8x = 56$ ↓ $2n = 8x = 56$
F. ananassa (strawberry)
$2n = 8x = 56$

(e) *Rubus vitifolius* (Californian blackberry) × *R. idaeus* (raspberry)
$2n = 8x = 56$ ↓ $2n = 2x = 14$
R. loganobaccus (loganberry)
$2n = 6x = 42$

(f) *Brassica campestris* (turnip) × *B. oleracea* (cabbage)
$2n = 2x = 20$ ↓ $2n = 2x = 18$
B. napus (swede and oil-seed rape)
$2n = 4x = 38$

All of the polyploid species above have arisen spontaneously and have subsequently been selected by mankind. All except the banana are fertile and are considered to be species in their own right because they do not easily hybridise with the parental species. The edible banana is triploid and although it forms fruits, the seeds inside remain undeveloped and the crop must be propagated asexually.

Since the discovery of a drug called **colchicine** which has the effect of doubling chromosome numbers, the creation of artificial polyploids has become relatively easy. In agriculture, one artificially produced allopolyploid has reached commercial importance. Durum wheat *Triticum turgidum* $(2n = 4x = 28)$ was crossed with rye *Secale cereale* $(2n = 2x = 14)$, resulting in a sterile F_1 hybrid. This was then treated with colchicine to induce chromosome doubling, so bringing about the creation of a fertile allopolyploid $(2n = 6x = 42)$, called **triticale** (pronounced triticaily or triticarly). The purpose in creating triticale was to try to combine the superior nutritional quality and yield of wheat with rye's winter hardiness and adaptation to sandy and acid soils. However, one cannot expect a 'raw' allopolyploid to show all the desired features because these are often the result of epistatic interactions in coadapted gene complexes. Nevertheless artificial selection in lines derived from the most promising hybrids has resulted in an economically viable crop plant adapted to poorer soils and a cooler climate.

3 Resistance to pesticides

Introduction

It has been estimated that approximately 35% of the world's potential food harvest is lost because of insect pests, diseases and weeds, and a further 10–20% of harvested food is destroyed by microorganisms, insects and rodents. These losses are in spite of the widespread use of pesticides. The development and application of chemical pesticides can be compared with research into new drugs; both have their associated limitations and problems, but few would deny their overall benefit to humanity.

Insects and insecticides (exercises 3.1 and 3.2)

Large scale use of insecticides began in 1941 with the introduction of the first synthetic organic insecticide, DDT. Before then, the number of insect species known to be resistant to natural insecticides like derris, nicotine and pyrethrum was fourteen. Forty years of widespread use of synthetic insecticides has increased this number to over 360 agricultural pests or vectors of disease.

The physiological basis of resistance to pesticides is known in some species. The mechanisms include the possession of enzymes which break down and therefore detoxify the chemical, avoidance of metabolic pathways blocked by the toxin, rapid excretion of the chemical, barriers to entry or even changes in behaviour. Genes play a part in all these mechanisms so it is not surprising to find that the genetic control of insecticide resistance is not the same in all species nor even in different populations of the same species.

From the published research it often appears that resistance is controlled by one or a few gene loci but this is likely to be an oversimplification of the real situation. Genes do not work in isolation; the product of one gene plays a part in the extremely complex dynamic network of metabolic pathways in a cell, where the enzymes involved are themselves all products of genes. A gene's effect on the phenotype therefore depends on the rest of the genotype, i.e. on the genetic background. A low level of resistance is often polygenically controlled. The contribution of major genes is over and above this base level, and because of their relatively large effects, their segregation results in observable Mendelian ratios.

Resistance is a quantitative character and presents some problems of measurement because an insect can be killed only once. Separate samples of insects are exposed to one of a range of doses and the numbers of dead insects are counted after exposure for a standard length of time. The percentage mortality is then plotted against dosage and the dosage which results in 50% mortality is read from the graph. This dose is called the LD50 (LD = lethal dose).

Genetics and biological control

Resistant insects are not necessarily completely immune to the toxic chemical but such large doses are required to kill them that the crop is damaged or the cost of treatment becomes uneconomic. Not only are many insecticides becoming less effective but there is growing concern over possible hazards associated with their use; risks to people using the chemicals, the effects of residues in food and disturbances of the ecosystem. A British Ministry of Agriculture report in 1964 recommended restrictions on the use of some pesticides.

If we are not to lose vast amounts of food to pests and diseases, some kind of control is necessary. An alternative to chemical control is the possibility of using natural predators and parasites. This latter method is known as biological control and is discussed further in the next chapter. There are other control measures which may also be called biological methods such as the breeding of plant varieties resistant to pests and diseases (see also exercise 2.2), the application of insect hormones to disrupt the life cycle of a pest and the release of genetically altered insects into a pest population. Whereas chemical control measures are applicable to most pests, the potential usefulness of biological methods is more restricted. A detailed knowledge of the biology of the pest is necessary for its weaknesses to be identified and exploited.

Genetic control is the employment of a pest species for its own control and the most outstanding example of its application is the screw worm fly (*Cochliomyia hominivorax*), a fly which lays its eggs in open wounds in domestic animals. In this control programme, large numbers of males were sterilised as pupae by exposure to gamma rays and the sterile males were liberated on the Caribbean island of Curaçao where screw worms were a serious problem. The female flies mate only once so those wild females which mated with irradiated males were effectively sterilised also. After twelve months of regular release of sterile males, no screw worms were found on domestic animals on the island. The same programme was employed in the southern USA but because cleared areas are continually recolonised from neighbouring populations, the programme must be an ongoing one.

Weeds and herbicides (exercise 3.3)

Resistance of weeds to herbicides is nowhere near such a problem as that of insects to insecticides. At least twelve different types of chemicals are used as herbicides and the effectiveness of only one group, the triazines, is being reduced because of resistance. Resistance to herbicides has been slower to appear probably because plants have a longer life cycle, are less mobile and are not as prolific as many insect pests. We already have a well stocked arsenal of herbicides and if a population evolves resistance to one, a suitable alternative is usually available, although perhaps at greater cost.

About thirty weed species can no longer be controlled by the triazine herbicides atrazine and simazine, but resistant populations are not widespread. Very few plant populations show any resistance to the commonly used herbicides 2,4-D and paraquat, probably because of their general toxic properties. Triazines are more specific; they bind to chloroplast thylakoid membranes and interfere with photosynthesis but resistant plants are able to prevent the triazine molecules from functioning. The physiological mechanisms of resistance to other herbicides include reduced absorption or translocation of the toxin, or increased rate of degradation, but the genetic control of resistance remains largely uninvestigated.

Fungi and fungicides (exercise 3.4)

In comparison to herbicides and insecticides, fungicides are the least widely used group of pesticides. Many diseases of crop plants are caused by parasitic fungi and the application of fungicides is often the only or at least the most economical method of control. Fungicides are used primarily to protect plants against infection rather than to cure plants already diseased. Many of them remain on the surface of the plant and kill or inhibit growth of the fungus before it can enter the plant's tissues. Resistance to fungicides such as these has rarely been recorded.

There has been available since the 1960s a wide variety of fungicides which enter the plant and which are translocated through it. These are known as **systemic fungicides** and have several advantages over the older ones: (1) they cure as well as prevent fungal diseases, (2) they are not easily washed away by rain, and (3) they are specific in their toxic effect on the fungus so are less likely to be toxic to the host plant or to other non-target organisms such as humans.

While specificity in its mode of action is a desirable feature of a fungicide, it is just this property which increases the probability that resistance will evolve. The non-systemic fungicides, such as those based on mercury or copper, act at many sites in cells as general enzyme inhibitors, while the systemic fungicides often act at a single site in the fungal cell. Mutation at only one gene locus may be sufficient to confer resistance. Resistance to a general toxin would require the accumulation of several mutations and the probability of their arising in the correct combination is very low. Prior to 1969 only seven species of fungi were known to be resistant to fungicides. In 1982, after widespread use of systemic fungicides, the number of resistant species had increased to over fifty.

Rodents and rodenticides (exercise 3.5)

One of the most thoroughly studied examples of resistance is that of rats to the poison warfarin. Warfarin is an anticoagulant and kills rodents by causing massive internal haemorrhages. It is widely used because in the dosages effective against rodents, it is relatively harmless to other animals. It was first used in Britain in 1953 to control rat and mouse infestations and was so effective that it was employed almost to the total exclusion of other poisons, but within five years resistant colonies were to be found in several parts of Britain as well as on the European continent and in the USA.

Conclusion

There is no doubt that resistance is a per-

petual problem to those trying to control pest species but it provides examples of evolution in action which are amenable to study and shows how well species can evolve in response to changes in their environment. Species which cannot adapt become extinct but despite all our attempts to exterminate pests, they continue to show just how adaptable they can be.

3.1 Resistance of flies to DDT

It is generally observed that when the same pesticide is used in an area for several years, the population to which it is directed evolves resistance. Three hypotheses concerning how this evolution may come about are:

Hypothesis 1. Continued exposure to low doses of the toxic agent causes the development of resistance in individual organisms. The resistance acquired during the life of an organism is inherited by its offspring. These acquire further resistance through continued exposure to the pesticide and so resistance is increased with succeeding generations.

Hypothesis 2. Genetic variation including alleles for pesticide resistance already exists in a population before any selective pressure is applied (i.e. before the pesticide is used). The appropriate alleles are rare. When selection pressure is applied, the few individuals carrying the rare alleles have on average more offspring than do susceptible ones. Thus the frequency of the allele(s) for resistance increases with each successive generation.

Hypothesis 3. Genes for pesticide resistance are not already present in an unexposed population but when the pesticide is used, the toxic agent itself causes the appropriate mutations to occur. The alleles for resistance then increase in frequency as a result of selection against individuals which do not carry them.

1 Which of the above hypotheses do you think is true?

One of these hypotheses was tested by an experiment using an outbred (genetically variable) population of the fruit fly, *Drosophila*. A male and a female fly were put into each of 50 culture tubes (vials) and each pair of flies produced about 200 offspring. The offspring from each pair were separated into two groups, A and B, making 50 group A and 50 group B vials. A piece of DDT impregnated paper was put into each of the group A vials and the percentage of flies killed was recorded for each one. The remaining group A flies were discarded. The group B flies which were the brothers and sisters of the group A flies showing the lowest mortality were used as parents for the next generation (see figure 3.1.1). This procedure was continued for 15 generations and the results are shown in figure 3.1.2.

Figure 3.1.1 *Breeding scheme for selection of flies resistant to DDT*

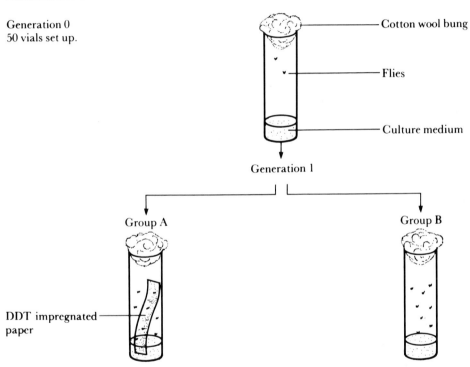

Generation 0
50 vials set up.

— Cotton wool bung

— Flies

— Culture medium

Generation 1

Group A

Group B

DDT impregnated paper

Half of the offspring from one pair of flies were exposed to DDT and mortality was recorded. Any survivors were discarded.

The other half of the offspring were untreated. If their brothers and sisters in group A showed low mortality the group B flies were divided into 50 vials and produced generation 2.

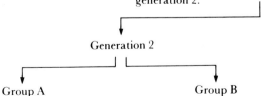

Generation 2

Group A

Group B

Treatment and selection as for generation 1

Figure 3.1.2 *Results of artificial selection for DDT resistance in* Drosophila

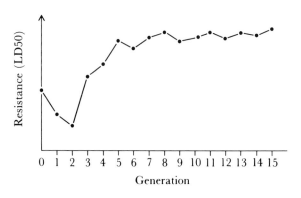

2 Which hypothesis, 1, 2 or 3, is supported by the results of this experiment?

3 Which one of the following is the best description of the genetic basis of the phenotypic variation?
  A Many gene loci each with small effect.
  B One gene locus with two alleles, the one for resistance being recessive.
  C One gene locus with two alleles, the one for resistance being dominant.

4 Explain carefully why selection was successful even though the selected flies were never exposed to DDT.

5 Suggest one reason to account for the observation that there is little further increase in resistance after generation 7.

3.2 Dieldrin resistance in the Australian sheep blowfly

Lucilia cuprina is a blowfly whose larvae feed on both carrion (dead animals) and live hosts. Female flies deposit eggs in the fleece of sheep and when the larvae hatch, they migrate to the skin surface and scrape at it with their mouth-parts, making a sore. More females are attracted to the wound to lay eggs there. Heavy infestations seriously damage the fleece and may even cause death of the sheep.

One method of control is application of the insecticide dieldrin by sheep dipping but some populations of *Lucilia* in Australia have become resistant. The genetics of resistance has been investigated by Shanahan who took a single resistant male fly and mated it to 10 susceptible females. The resulting F_1 generation was tested for dieldrin resistance and the results are shown in figure 3.2.1 together with the results of similar tests on a resistant and a susceptible strain. Notice that the axes in figure 3.2.1 are not on a linear scale. The percentages are on a probability scale and the dosages are on a logarithmic scale. The use of these scales makes the plot of percentage mortality against dosage lie on a straight line. These lines are called dosage–mortality lines.

Figure 3.2.1 *Dieldrin dosage–mortality lines for a resistant and a susceptible strain of* Lucilia cuprina *and an F_1 generation.*

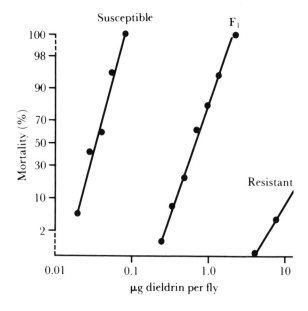

1 What information is conveyed by the gradient of a dosage–mortality line?

2 Describe the degree of resistance in the F_1 flies compared with the susceptible and resistant parent strains.

The results for the F_1 generation do not allow us to make a definite statement about the number of gene loci involved in determining resistance. Dosage–mortality lines for backcross generations give more information about the genetic control. Shanahan backcrossed F_1 flies to the susceptible strain and treated the offspring with 0.1 μg dieldrin per fly. The survivors were again backcrossed to the susceptible strain and the progeny were selected in the same way. This was continued for six generations and the dosage–mortality line for the sixth backcross generation is shown in figure 3.2.2.

Figure 3.2.2 *Dieldrin dosage mortality line in a sixth backcross generation.*

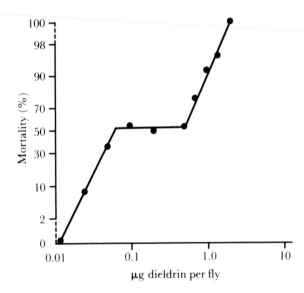

μg dieldrin per fly

3 Why was a dose of 0.1 μg dieldrin per fly used in the selection of the backcross progeny rather than a higher or lower dose?

4 How do the results for the sixth backcross generation support the hypothesis of single gene control of dieldrin resistance in *Lucilia cuprina*?

After resistance to dieldrin had been diagnosed in 1957, the insecticide used in sheep

dips was changed. Table 3.2.1 shows the mean frequency of the allele for resistance measured four times since the cessation of the use of this insecticide.

Table 3.2.1 *Frequency of the allele for resistance to dieldrin in an Australian population of* Lucilia cuprina

Year	Frequency
1958–59	0.42
1959–60	0.30
1971–72	0.06
1972–73	0.04

5 Using the Hardy–Weinberg formula, calculate the percentage of flies which would be resistant (to a dose of 0.1 μg dieldrin) in 1958–59 and in 1972–73.

6 Explain in general terms why the allele for resistance has declined in frequency over the fourteen year period.

3.3 Herbicide resistance

The resistance of weeds to herbicides is a relatively minor problem in comparison to resistance in other pests but for individual farmers and horticulturalists, the eradication of persistent weeds is of considerable economic importance.

Triazine resistant groundsel (*Senecio vulgaris*) infests a quarter of a million hectares of arable land in western Washington, USA, and by 1982 resistant populations of this species had been reported from seven localities in Britain. Genetic variation conferring resistance had apparently occurred by mutation independently in several different areas. Once it has occurred, the appropriate gene or genes will increase in frequency as long as there is continued selection pressure from the herbicide.

1 Generally, weed species which have evolved resistance to herbicides
(a) are annuals, some having more than two generations per year;
(b) show a high degree of self-fertility;
(c) have high fecundity (produce a very large number of seeds).
Explain how each of the characteristics (a), (b) and (c) contributes to rapid evolution of herbicide resistance.

In a weed species of grass, *Poa annua*, the inheritance of resistance to triazine herbicides follows the inheritance of the cytoplasm. In resistant plants, it is the chloroplasts which are modified and a plant inherits its chloroplasts from its mother. Inheritance through the cytoplasm of the mother rather than through the genes contributed in the nuclei of both gametes is called **maternal inheritance**. It is possible but not certain that triazine resistance is a consequence of mutation of the chloroplast DNA rather than of the nuclear DNA.

2 What is the expected ratio of resistant:susceptible offspring in the following crosses?
(a) Resistance is controlled by a dominant gene in the nucleus.
  (i) A heterozygous resistant female × a homozygous recessive susceptible male.
  (ii) The reciprocal cross.
(b) Resistance is controlled by the chloroplasts.
  (i) A resistant female × a susceptible male.
  (ii) The reciprocal cross.

Imagine that the female plant in question 2(a)(i) and the female plant in question 2(b)(i) are transported to two different plant nurseries, A and B respectively. The species is an annual which dies after setting seed. Both plants are self-fertilised and each produces 100 seeds all of which germinate the following spring. Both nurseries are sprayed with herbicide and all susceptible plants are killed. In your answers to questions 3 and 4 assume that

the numbers observed are those expected according to Mendelian ratios.

3 How many resistant offspring will remain in each of the nurseries?

4 Each of the surviving plants again fertilises itself and produces 100 progeny. How many resistant plants will there now be in each of the two nurseries (assuming no immigration of plants from outside the nursery)?

5 If a mutation conferring resistance occurs only once, describe how it could be carried to other areas if it is
(a) in the cytoplasm (chloroplast),
(b) in the nucleus.

6 Using your answers to questions 4 and 5, explain how maternal inheritance of herbicide resistance can be
(a) advantageous and
(b) disadvantageous to the spread of resistance.

3.4 The mechanism of benomyl resistance in a fungus

As a general rule, a gene locus can be identified in an organism only when alternative alleles of the gene exist. Unless there is variation at the locus, it is difficult to determine its existence by conventional breeding experiments. All eukaryotes (organisms higher than bacteria and blue green algae) contain a globular protein called **tubulin** which makes up the microtubules in centrioles, cilia, flagella and the mitotic spindle. Each molecule of tubulin is composed of two polypeptides called α-tubulin and β-tubulin. Many molecules of both kinds polymerise in a regular fashion to form a cylindrical microtubule. The work described in this exercise was the first report of the identification of a gene for β-tubulin. The work is significant also in that it demonstrates how an investigation into a problem of economic importance has led to advancement in our understanding of molecular biology.

The systemic fungicide benomyl owes its fungicidal action to its ability to bind to β-tubulin so preventing it from polymerising and forming microtubules. Consequently no spindle can form and the fungal cells cannot divide. The tubulin of the host plant is not affected in the same way. Resistance to benomyl can evolve quickly. In some instances, resistant populations of disease-causing fungi have been reported within a few months of first spraying with benomyl. In the fungus *Aspergillus nidulans*, high resistance to benomyl is conferred by a single gene known as *ben-A* which prevents benomyl from binding to β-tubulin. Sheir-Neiss and her colleagues obtained a susceptible wild type strain of *A. nidulans* and several resistant strains from various localities, each different from the wild type at the *ben-A* locus. *Aspergillus nidulans* is haploid. Table 3.4.1 shows the dose of benomyl in $\mu g\ cm^{-3}$ of culture medium which reduces growth of the fungus by 50% (the ED50).

Table 3.4.1 *Resistance of wild type and 15 resistant strains of* Aspergillus nidulans *to benomyl*

Strain	ED50	Strain	ED50
wild type	0.8	R-11	8
R-1	24	R-13	30
R-2	6	R-15	8
R-3	15	R-16	24
R-4	7	R-20	6
R-7	6	R-22	15
R-9	8	R-23	10
R-10	8	R-25	6

1 There is some evidence from table 3.4.1 that the gene at the *ben-A* locus is not the same allele in the different resistant strains. Estimate the minimum number of alleles for resistance assuming that the ED50 for each strain may vary by up to 1 microgram either side of the value given in the table.

The investigators labelled all the proteins in the *A. nidulans* strains using radioactive sulphur so that the proteins could be located by autoradiography, and then they used two-way electrophoresis to separate them (see also exercise 2.5). In two-way electrophoresis, the proteins are first run through a gel in one direction, then the gel is turned through 90° and run again. This gives better separation of proteins in the mixture. From previous experiments they knew which spots on the gel contained β-tubulin. Figure 3.4.1 represents the tubulin-containing region of the gel from the wild type and three of the resistant strains. The proteins were run first from bottom to top and then from left to right as indicated by the arrows. Other, non-tubulin proteins are shown in the diagrams. All the protein molecules have an overall (net) charge and after further experiments it was concluded that the mutant β-tubulins differed from wild type by one extra negative charge (1^-), one extra positive charge (1^+) or two extra positive charges (2^+).

Figure 3.4.1 *Diagrams of the distribution on electrophoresis gels of β-tubulin (shaded) and non-tubulin proteins of wild type and three benomyl resistant strains of* Aspergillus nidulans

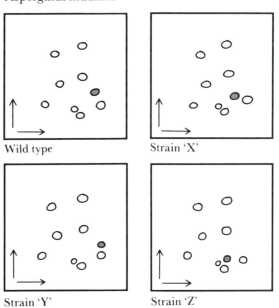

Wild type   Strain 'X'

Strain 'Y'   Strain 'Z'

2 Compare the position of β-tubulin in the gels in figure 3.4.1 for wild type and three resistant strains 'X', 'Y' and 'Z'. Which resistant strain, X, Y or Z has β-tubulin with
(a) one extra positive charge,
(b) two extra positive charges,
(c) one extra negative charge?

3 Use your knowledge of the ionisation of proteins and state whether the buffer used during electrophoresis, in both directions, had a higher or lower pH than the isoelectric point of wild type β-tubulin. Explain your answer.

The extra charges on the mutant β-tubulin molecules are thought to be the result of amino acid substitutions. These substitutions perhaps occur at the benomyl–tubulin binding site, so preventing the fungicide from binding with tubulin. The function of the tubulin is therefore not inhibited in the resistant strains. Table 3.4.2 shows the changes in charge, if any, of the β-tubulins of the resistant strains compared with the wild type.

Table 3.4.2   *Differences in charge on mutant β-tubulins compared with wild type*

Strain	Extra charge		Strain	Extra charge
R-1	none		R-11	1^+
R-2	1^-		R-13	1^-
R-3	none		R-15	none
R-4	1^-		R-16	none
R-7	1^-		R-20	2^+
R-9	none		R-22	1^-
R-10	1^-		R-23	1^-
			R-25	1^-

4 Table 3.4.2 shows that some of the tubulins in the resistant strains have the same charge as wild type tubulin yet benomyl does not bind to them. Explain what the change or changes in the mutant tubulins may be.

5 What is the minimum number of base pairs which must be altered at the *ben-A* locus to bring about substitution of a single amino acid?

6 Your answer to question 1 was based on the differences in the dosage of benomyl required to reduce growth. Use the information in both tables 3.4.1 and 3.4.2 to make a new estimate of the number of mutant alleles.

This investigation identified the *ben-A* locus as a structural gene for β-tubulin. The results show that mutation at several different sites within the gene can give rise to benomyl resistance. In other words, several different changes in the structure of the β-tubulin protein can prevent benomyl binding to it.

7 Explain how this finding is consistent with the observation that benomyl resistance in a wild fungus population can appear very quickly, within a matter of months, after first application of the fungicide.

In Britain, resistance to benomyl is common in the fungi causing eyespot disease in wheat and barley and septoria disease of wheat.

3.5 *Resistance of rodents to warfarin*

Warfarin is an anticoagulant drug used both as a treatment for thrombosis in humans and as an overdose to kill rodent pests such as rats and mice. Warfarin works by interfering with the normal blood clotting mechanism which is constantly called upon in the repair of spontaneous leakages from small blood vessels. In the absence of a rapid clotting mechanism, a mammal will die from internal haemorrhages.

The blood clotting process is a very complex one involving at least thirteen factors. Four of these, including prothrombin, depend on vitamin K for their activation or production and warfarin inhibits the activity of an enzyme (vitamin K oxide reductase) involved in vitamin K metabolism. In rats resistant to warfarin, this enzyme has an altered structure so it can still function although less effectively than the normal enzyme. From the rat's point of view, it is better to have an enzyme that works inefficiently than one that does not work at all, but it means that animals having the altered enzyme need more vitamin K for their blood to clot normally.

An attempt was made to transfer warfarin resistance into tame laboratory rats because wild rats are fierce and awkward to handle in the laboratory. A resistant wild male was crossed to several warfarin susceptible, tame females and 28 out of 60 progeny were resistant. When resistant progeny were crossed to tame rats of the same kind as their mother, half of their offspring were resistant.

1 How do these results suggest that a single gene locus determines resistance?

2 Without using symbols, describe the genotype of the original resistant wild male rat.

3 Is the allele for resistance dominant or recessive?

The allele for resistance is called Rw^2 and the wild type allele is called Rw^1. Table 3.5.1 shows the vitamin K requirements of rats with the three genotypes.

Table 3.5.1   *Vitamin K requirements of warfarin resistant and susceptible rats*

Genotype	Resistance to warfarin	Vitamin K requirement (μg/100 g body weight per day)
Rw^1/Rw^1	susceptible	6.0
Rw^1/Rw^2	resistant	6.0
Rw^2/Rw^2	resistant	80.0

4 Is Rw^2 dominant or recessive in its effects on vitamin K requirement?

Your answers to questions 3 and 4 (if correct) demonstrate an important concept in genetics; dominance and recessivity are not properties of the alleles themselves but are descrip-

tions of the relationships between alleles. Here we have an allele, Rw^2, which affects the phenotype in two ways; it confers both resistance to warfarin and an increased requirement for vitamin K. In one effect it is dominant and in the other it is recessive to Rw^1. When both forms of the vitamin K oxide reductase enzyme are present in the same animal, as they are in the heterozygote, resistance to warfarin is conferred without raising the requirement for the vitamin. Homozygous Rw^2Rw^2 rats, although resistant to warfarin, will also die from internal bleeding if they have insufficient dietary vitamin K.

In a normal population where Rw^2 is present, there may be selection against Rw^1Rw^1 by farmers using warfarin and against Rw^2Rw^2 due to a shortage of the vitamin in the diet. The animals producing the most offspring will be Rw^1Rw^2 whose progeny will include homozygotes of both kinds. The warfarin resistance/susceptibility polymorphism will be maintained in a state of balance because of the superiority of the heterozygotes.

A study was made of wild rats on farms around Welshpool where resistance was first discovered in 1959. At the time of the study the incidence of resistance in this area was steady. Rats were trapped and their genotypes were determined (table 3.5.2).

Table 3.5.2   *Genotypes of wild rats on farms around Welshpool*

Genotype	Rw^1Rw^1	Rw^1Rw^2	Rw^2Rw^2	Total
Phenotype	susceptible	resistant	resistant	
Number caught	28	42	4	74

5 Using the Hardy–Weinberg equation and the figures in table 3.5.2, calculate the expected number of rats captured with each genotype.

6 Use the chi-square test to determine whether differences between observed and expected numbers are statistically significant (χ^2 has one degree of freedom). Is there any evidence that the heterozygotes are at an advantage?

7 Calculate the observed number of rats of each homozygous genotype as a percentage of the expected number of that genotype. Which homozygote appears to be at the greatest disadvantage?

A further investigation was carried out in a nearby area where warfarin was also used until 1973. In that year nearly 60% of rats in the area were resistant. The use of warfarin was stopped and in 1975, the incidence of resistance was found to be less than 40%.

8 Account for the decline in the percentage of resistant rats when the use of warfarin was discontinued.

Many populations of mice are also resistant to warfarin. In fact, in urban areas, mice have replaced rats as the major pest. Although the genetic basis of resistance in mice was investigated, its nature proved difficult to establish. It now appears that resistance is conferred by a dominant gene but that other genes modify its expression. A similar phenomenon occurs in rats; Rw^2 has effects large enough to be recognised but genes elsewhere in the chromosomes also contribute to the observed phenotype. In the mouse, these modifier genes exert a relatively major effect such that the genetic basis of warfarin resistance in the mouse may be described as polygenic. Polygenic inheritance means that many gene loci are involved in bringing about phenotypic variation in a character (see exercise 1.1). The contribution made by each locus will vary in extent. In the mouse, one locus has a relatively large effect and others contribute substantially to it while in the rat, modifier genes make only a small contribution when compared with the effect of the 'Rw' locus.

4 Resistance to pests and diseases

Introduction

Plant diseases may be classified into those caused by parasites such as viruses, bacteria and fungi and those caused by environmental factors such as mineral deficiencies, unfavourable temperatures and injurious chemicals. While viruses and bacteria are the most common disease-causing organisms (**pathogens**) in animals, the predominant pathogens of plants are fungi.

Coevolution of host and parasite

Most plants are immune to most diseases and owe their complete resistance to such factors as mechanical barriers to infection or total physiological incompatibility. Within a species there may be variation between individuals in susceptibility to potential pathogens but whether a plant is regarded as resistant or susceptible to a disease depends on the standards used for comparison. In the potato for instance, cultivated plants classed as resistant to the blight fungus (*Phytophthora infestans*) will often show some signs of disease while those more seriously affected would be called susceptible. However, even these susceptible plants show some degree of resistance when compared with certain wild varieties.

In chapter 3 we saw how pests evolve resistance to pesticides by natural selection acting on genetic variation in the population. Evolution of resistance makes it necessary for us to devise ever more effective measures against the pests. We cannot stop the development of new pesticides if we wish to remain one step ahead of our adversaries. Likewise, by the process of natural selection, plants evolve resistance to their parasites, and the parasites evolve resistance to the defences of their hosts. Host and parasite evolve together; they **coevolve** because the one continually exerts changing selection pressures on the other. This phenomenon might be what the Red Queen had in mind in Lewis Carroll's *Through the Looking Glass* when she said to Alice, '. . . it takes all the running you can do to keep in the same place. If you want to go somewhere else, you must run at least twice as fast as that.' Every student of evolution learns that organisms adapt to their environment but what is commonly overlooked is that the environment of a species includes its predators, prey and parasites, all of which are also evolving. Evolutionary biologists call the idea that a species evolves as a result of maintaining adaptation to an ever-changing environment, the **Red Queen hypothesis**.

Figure 4.1 *Alice with the Red Queen*

A **virulent** pathogen is one which is able to infect and reproduce in the host, thereby causing disease. A pathogen is called **avirulent** either if it is unable to infect a potential host or if it causes only mild disease symptoms. Coevolution over a long period of time has resulted in a state of dynamic equilibrium between host and parasite. Rarely do the defences of the host species become so effective as to prevent the pathogen from reproducing at all and neither does a pathogen normally cause such severe disease that the host species becomes extinct, a strategy which would be suicidal for the parasite. Sometimes the balance is disturbed, giving rise to disease epidemics. A recent example is Dutch Elm disease caused by the fungus *Ceratocystis ulmi* which is threatening the English Elm with extinction. As this tree reproduces vegetatively by root suckers and rarely sets seed, there is little genetic variation in the species, making the evolution of resistance unlikely.

Genetics of resistance to plant pathogens (exercises 4.1 and 4.2)

Both host and pathogen show genetic variation in susceptibility and virulence respectively. Whether a particular pathogen can cause disease in a particular plant depends on two factors, the susceptibility/resistance of the plant and the virulence/avirulence of the pathogen. Table 4.1 shows that only one combination of genotypes results in disease.

Table 4.1   *Host–parasite interactions*

	Parasite	
Host	Virulent	Avirulent
resistant	no disease	no disease
susceptible	disease	no disease

Different **races** of pathogens exist, each one carrying different genes for virulence. The host responds to the new selection pressure and in time a new gene for resistance evolves. The notion that for each virulence gene in the pathogen there is a corresponding resistance gene in the host is known as the **gene for gene hypothesis**. The new genes may be alleles at the same locus as an 'old' one or may be at loci not previously associated with resistance or virulence. Plant varieties possessing certain alleles for resistance are more resistant to some races of the pathogen than to others, i.e. they show specific resistance. This is also described as 'vertical' resistance from the shape of the graph representing it (figure 4.2). When a plant variety is fairly equally resistant to most races of the pathogen, it is called 'horizontal' or general resistance and is probably polygenically determined. Vertical resistance is likely to be observed if host and pathogen show a gene for gene pattern of evolution.

Figure 4.2 *'Vertical' and 'horizontal' resistance. The graph shows the resistance of two varieties of plant, A and B, to five races of a pathogen*

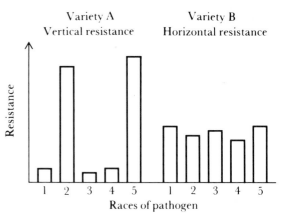

Plant breeders can aid evolution in the crop by deliberately introducing resistance genes from other cultivated varieties or even wild relatives of the cultivated crop (see also exercise 2.2). Ideally, plant breeders should be aiming for horizontal resistance which would be more permanent but it is very much more difficult to transfer many genes, each with small effect (polygenes), from one variety into another than to transfer single alleles with a major effect.

Exercise 2.8 described the utilization of cytoplasmically determined male sterility in the breeding of hybrid corn. By 1970, 85% of hybrid corn grown in the USA had this kind of cytoplasm. It is now known that the male sterility factor is carried by the mitochondrial DNA together with a mitochondrial gene which determines susceptibility to race T of *Helminthosporium maydis*, the causative agent of southern corn leaf blight. The cytoplasmic uniformity of maize in the southern United States led, in 1970, to one of the most damaging and widely dispersed epidemics in the history of plant pathology. The dangers of genetic uniformity are well known but it took an epidemic to make plant breeders realise that mitochondrial (and chloroplast) genes cannot be ignored.

Resistance to pests (exercises 4.3 and 4.4)

Plants provide food not only for humans and parasitic microorganisms but also for herbivorous animals including insect, nematode and mollusc pests which reduce the yield of our crop plants. Instead of using chemical pesticides we may be able to exploit the plants' own capabilities of discouraging herbivores. Morphological deterrents include thorns, spines and stinging hairs as protection against larger animals and a hairy epidermis is effective against many insect pests.

Plants synthesise compounds called **secondary metabolites** such as alkaloids, glycosides, acids and steroids which act as defence mechanisms. These may discourage insects from biting, or are toxic and kill the insects before serious damage is done. Such useful drugs as caffeine, quinine, cocaine, opium, atropine and digitalin all owe their origin to protection against herbivores.

Plants possessing chemical deterrents are often also unsuitable as food for humans. Vegetable oil made from oil-seed rape used to contain potentially harmful levels of erucic acid but varieties are now grown which have been selected for low erucic acid content.

Highly nutritious legumes include peas, beans, peanuts, lentils, clover and alfalfa but lupins and laburnum are poisonous (see also exercise 2.5). In India there is a legume cultivated for food which will grow in the poorest soils but it contains a nerve poison. If non-toxic plants could be bred, some of the poorest people in India would not be forced to make the choice between hunger and paralysis. Cotton seed is another example of a potentially valuable food source being made unavailable by toxins. Like legumes, cotton seeds are a rich source of protein but there is a toxic substance called **gossypol** distributed throughout the cotton plant. Gossypol-free varieties have been bred but, deprived of their natural insect deterrent, these plants are considerably more vulnerable to pests.

Using disease organisms to control pests (exercise 4.5)

Whereas a disease epidemic in an economically important crop may be disastrous for the farmer, the same capacity of a pathogen for rapid increase can be exploited to attack a species which is itself a pest. Diseases caused by bacteria and viruses have been deliberately used to control pests like pine sawfly larvae in Canada and rabbits in Australia. Exploitation of a parasite or predator to reduce the numbers of a pest species is called **biological control**.

Whether we regard a species as a friend or foe makes little difference to the natural selection of resistance to disease. We might attempt to hasten the evolution of resistance in an economic crop but we can do little to prevent it also occurring in a pest species subjected to biological control. By deliberately introducing a virulent disease into a pest population, we are creating new environments for both pest and pathogen. Both will evolve; they will coevolve, with the virulence of the pathogen decreasing and the resistance of the host increasing until both species are adapted to each other. As far as we are concerned, the effectiveness of the biological control shows a decline, but then natural selection is blind to the wishes of humanity. The more we know about genetics, evolution and natural selection, the more accurately we shall be able to predict and manipulate the course of events.

4.1 Controlling powdery mildew of barley

Powdery mildew (*Erysiphe graminis hordei*) is a parasitic fungus which overwinters as a mass of hyphae (a mycelium) on barley leaves and in the spring produces haploid asexual spores. These are carried by the wind to leaves of young barley plants where they germinate. Infected plants show reduced yield and in the UK, where the disease is common, losses may be 20% or more. Barley must be protected with fungicide if it is to be economically viable but cultivars (cultivated varieties) showing some resistance to *Erysiphe graminis hordei* have been selectively bred.

Even a resistant crop will not be entirely free of the parasite. Barley has at least 17 genes conferring resistance but whenever a new resistance gene is introduced into a barley cultivar its effectiveness is lost within about three or four years, not because of any change in the barley but because the pathogen acquires a new gene by mutation. This new gene allows it to overcome the resistance conferred by the barley gene. The relatively rapid response by the pathogen is a consequence of its short life cycle, the production of huge numbers of spores and the fact that the fungus is haploid.

1 If 10^{13} spores are produced per hectare per day and the mutation rate per gene locus is 10^{-8}, approximately how many spores per hectare per day would carry a new mutant allele at a particular locus?

2 Why do the following allow rapid evolution of virulence?

(a) The production of large numbers of spores.
(b) The haploid nature of the fungus.

3 Because barley is a self-fertilising species, each cultivar consists of genetically identical plants. Explain why this will encourage the rapid spread of a virulent pathogen.

Plant pathologists are now recommending that farmers should grow a crop of barley which is a mixture of several different cultivars, each one carrying different genes for resistance. The cultivars used are matched for simultaneous ripening and seeds of three of them are mixed before sowing. Table 4.1.1 shows the results of an experiment to discover whether mixtures of three cultivars yielded more grain than each cultivar grown alone, that is, in monoculture. The seeds were sown at the same density in both sets of plots.

Table 4.1.1   *Yields of barley cultivars grown alone or in mixtures*

Name of cultivar	Yield of cultivar when grown in monoculture (tonnes/hectare)	Yield of mixtures containing cultivar (tonnes/hectare)
Sundance	4.78	5.05
Georgie	4.65	5.10
Athos	4.70	5.09
Mazurka	4.69	5.14
Maris Mink	4.63	4.97
Ark Royal	4.71	5.09

4 (a) What is the average yield of cultivars grown in monoculture?
(b) What is the average yield of mixtures of cultivars?
(c) What is the percentage increase in yield when cultivars are grown in mixtures?
(d) If Sundance, Maris Mink and Ark Royal are grown together in a mixture, what would be the expected yield in tonnes/hectare?

The increase in yield is largely due to decreased levels of disease, even in susceptible plants. Mildew populations consist of a large number of different races but if the components of a mixed crop of barley are carefully chosen, one-third, two-thirds or all the plants in the field will be resistant to the prevalent race or races of the pathogen. This means that not only will there be fewer spores, but their distribution from a site of infection will be inhibited by the presence of resistant plants.

4.2 Resistance to fungal diseases in rubber and tobacco

Resistance of a plant to a fungal pathogen is rarely of an all or nothing type; even resistant plants show varying degrees of susceptibility. This exercise concerns the variation in resistance to disease in rubber trees and tobacco plants.

Genetically heterogeneous (mixed) rubber trees in a plantation were inspected for infection by *Gloeosporium* leaf disease. Each tree was assigned to one of eight categories according to the degree of infection shown. Category 1 represents the most susceptible trees and category 8 represents the most resistant ones. Table 4.2.1 shows the percentage of trees in each category.

The results of a similar investigation into blue mould disease in tobacco are given in table 4.2.2. Two populations of plants were

inspected for resistance, one was a resistant inbred strain and the other was an F_2 generation derived from crossing the resistant inbred strain to a susceptible inbred strain and then allowing the progeny to self-fertilise.

1 (a) Plot a histogram of the results for the rubber trees.
   (b) Plot histograms for each set of results for the tobacco plants.

2 Account for the observed phenotypic variation in the population of rubber trees.

3 Each inbred strain of tobacco is genetically homogeneous (the same) as far as resistance genes are concerned. The plants in the susceptible inbred strain used in the cross described above were all in categories 1 or 2. Over 90% of the F_1 plants were in categories 5 or 6 and the results for the F_2 generation are shown in table 4.2.2. What is the minimum number of gene loci which could account for these results? Explain your answer.

4.3 Resistance of rice to whitebacked planthopper

There are about twenty species of insect which are major pests of rice. Planthoppers pierce stems or leaves with their mouthparts and suck the contents of the phloem. Their feeding directly damages the crop but perhaps of

Table 4.2.1   *Resistance of a population of rubber trees to leaf disease* (Gloeosporium)

Category	1 (susceptible)	2	3	4	5	6	7	8 (resistant)
Percentage of plants	0	1.5	10.6	31.8	33.3	18.2	3.0	1.5

Table 4.2.2   *Resistance of an inbred and an F_2 population of tobacco plants to blue mould* (Peronospora tabacina)

Category	1 (susceptible)	2	3	4	5	6 (resistant)	
Percentage of plants	0.2	0.8	0.2	0.6	4.2	94.0	Resistant inbred strain
	8.9	18.9	2.7	4.8	22.7	42.0	F_2 generation

greater importance is the fact that they are often vectors of virus diseases. Breeding rice varieties which are resistant to the insect pests is one of the aims of the International Rice Research Institute (IRRI) in the Philippines. There, Nair, Masajo and Khush investigated 21 varieties of rice known to be resistant to the whitebacked planthopper *Sogatella furcifera*. They discovered that the genetics of resistance is straightforward.

All the varieties of rice were crossed to a susceptible variety 'TN1' and in every case the F_1 plants were resistant. The F_1 plants were selfed and table 4.3.1 shows the results for the F_2 generation for two of the varieties.

Table 4.3.1   *Resistance of F_2 generations to planthoppers*

F_2 generation from	Resistant	Susceptible
'TN1' × '293'	242	78
'TN1' × '65'	222	45

1 What is the nearest Mendelian ratio which fits the F_2 data for the 'TN1' × '293' cross?

2 How many gene loci control the difference in resistance between 'TN1' and '293'?

3 In order to check their conclusions concerning the genetic control of resistance, the investigators allowed the resistant F_2 plants from the 'TN1' × '293' cross to self-fertilise and produce F_3 families. If their conclusions were correct, what proportion of the F_3 families should include susceptible plants? (These are called segregating families.)

4 The F_2 data for the 'TN1' × '65' cross fit a two gene locus model because they agree with a Mendelian ratio of $13:3$. Use the symbols *A*, *a*, *B* and *b*, where *A* is an allele for resistance. Define the phenotypic effects of the other alleles and give the genotypes of the susceptible F_2 plants. (Hint: Use a Punnett square.)

5 Resistant plants from the 'TN1' × '65' cross were self-fertilised and F_3 families raised. What proportion of the resistant F_2 plants would give rise to segregating F_3 families?

4.4 Resistance of cotton to pests

The caterpillar of the moth *Heliothis virescens* is known as the tobacco budworm and feeds on all parts of cotton (and tobacco) plants but especially on the flower buds. Cotton (*Gossypium hirsutum*) contains a poisonous compound, gossypol, and it has been suggested that cotton plants with high gossypol content could be bred to resist attacks by insects such as the tobacco budworm.

In the cotton plant, two gene loci determining the presence or absence of glands containing gossypol are known as 'G' and 'H'. Plants with the genotype *gg hh* have no glands and contain very little of the poison. In an investigation of the possible deterrent effect of gossypol, Wilson and Shaver obtained plants with different combinations of dominant and recessive alleles at the 'G' and 'H' loci and measured the gossypol content of the seedlings. Budworms were allowed to feed on the seedlings for a standard length of time and the amount of damage done was measured on a

Table 4.4.1   *Seedling gossypol content and damage by budworms*

Genotype	Seedling gossypol content (%)	Seedling damage (see text)
GG HH	0.73	2.21
GG hh	0.42	3.33
gg HH	0.28	3.47
gg hh	0.09	4.20
GG Hh	0.57	3.00
Gg HH	0.60	2.95
Gg Hh	0.38	3.79
Gg hh	0.13	4.19
gg Hh	0.11	4.00

scale of 1 (least damage) to 5 (most damage). Twenty-four seedlings of each genotype group were exposed to two budworms each and the results are shown in table 4.4.1.

1 Plot a scatter diagram to show the relationship between gossypol content of seedlings and damage done by budworms. Describe the relationship.

2 (a) Compare the gossypol content of two suitable genotypes selected from table 4.4.1 to illustrate why it is that allele *G* is not truly dominant to allele *g*.
  (b) Similarly, show how allele *H* is not truly dominant to allele *h*.

3 Genotype *gg hh* has no 'dominant' genes for gossypol and the smallest percentage of gossypol, while *GG HH* has four 'dominant' genes and the greatest percentage of gossypol. What is the mean gossypol content of genotypes having
  (a) one 'dominant' gene,
  (b) two 'dominant' genes,
  (c) three 'dominant' genes?

4 Plot a graph to show how mean gossypol content varies with number of 'dominant' genes present.

In the graph for question 4, the points nearly all lie on a straight line. This means that the genes are acting additively (see exercise 1.5). Additional 'dominant' genes each add to gossypol content by the same amount.

From the relationship you found in your scatter diagram (question 1), it is tempting to suppose that the budworms are eating less because of the presence of the toxin but this evidence is insufficient to allow us to infer a causal relationship. The budworms may be responding to something else in the plants which is also correlated with gossypol content. However, further investigations with budworms raised on an artificial medium containing different amounts of gossypol have shown that feeding rate and growth of larvae are indeed inhibited by the toxin.

In view of the budworm's capacity to evolve insecticide resistance, Raulston and colleagues decided to investigate whether the insects could evolve resistance to gossypol. They collected budworm caterpillars from a cotton plantation and reared them on an artificial medium in the laboratory. Half of the caterpillars had gossypol added to their diet; this was the selected line. The other half had the same diet but without gossypol; this was the control line. The growth of all the caterpillars in the selected line was inhibited by gossypol and resistance was selected for by choosing as parents of the next generation, only the heaviest adult moths which had been reared on the gossypol medium. Selection was continued for thirteen generations. No selection was carried out on the control line. Response to selection was estimated by comparing selected and control lines on various measures of the pupa (chrysalis) stage. Table 4.4.2 gives the weight of pupae in both control and selected lines over thirteen generations.

5 What effect did gossypol have on the weight of pupae in the first three generations of the experiment?

Table 4.4.2 *Mean weight of budworm pupae (in mg) in a line selected for tolerance to gossypol and in a control line*

Generation	Selected	Control
1	205*	294
2	224*	283
3	216*	269
4	255	272
5	275	274
6	279	281
7	263	277
8	287	280
9	288	278
10	272	275
11	275	274
12	286	288
13	303	287

* The difference in mean weight between control and selected lines is significant at the 5% level of probability.

6 How do you account for the observation that there is no significant difference in mean weight of pupae from the fourth generation of selection even though the selected caterpillars have gossypol in their diet?

As the budworms responded to selection, more gossypol was incorporated into their diet. By the thirteenth generation, the gossypol content was equivalent to a level in the plant of 2%.

7 Compare this figure of 2% with the figures in table 4.4.1. In the light of the results of the selection experiment, do you think that resistance to budworm damage could be achieved by breeding plants with a high gossypol content?

8 What do the results of the selection experiment suggest to you about the presence of genetic variation for gossypol resistance in the wild population of *Heliothis virescens*?

4.5 Myxomatosis in Australian rabbits

In the 1950s the rabbit disease myxomatosis devastated rabbit populations in Australia and Europe. Its introduction into Australia was the beginning of a programme of biological control. The rabbit itself was an introduction into Australia from Europe and had multiplied to such an extent that it was successfully competing with sheep for pasture grasses and severely reducing the profitability of sheep farms.

Myxomatosis was first recognised in a laboratory rabbit colony in South America in 1896. Nearly fifty years later, it was shown that the myxoma virus is present in populations of the common wild rabbit, the tapeti, of Brazil where it causes nothing more serious than a small skin tumour. The virus is carried from one host to another by mosquitoes whose mouthparts become contaminated when they pierce through infected skin to feed on the

rabbit's blood. When the same virus infects the European rabbit, the disease is much more severe. The head becomes very swollen and skin tumours occur all over the body. The animal dies within about two weeks of infection.

After research had confirmed that myxomatosis is confined to rabbits, the disease was released in south-eastern Australia in 1950. It spread at the rate of about 100 miles per week mainly in the vicinity of the Murray–Darling river system. In 1951 myxomatosis was introduced into the western states but its failure to spread there was considered to be related to the more arid conditions of the west.

The rabbit mortality rate in the east in 1950–51 was about 99.5% but declined to about 30% in seven years. By 1959 rabbit numbers were on the increase again and it was clear that myxomatosis alone was not going to solve Australia's rabbit problem.

The mortality rate dropped for three reasons; the rabbits evolved resistance to the disease, the virus became less virulent and females which had recovered from myxomatosis passed on antibodies across the placenta and in their milk, so giving passive immunity to their young.

In order to test whether rabbits were evolving genetically determined resistance, a number of wild caught uninfected rabbits were inoculated with a standard strain of virus. This strain was obtained in 1953, kept at low temperatures, and used for inoculating test animals over the next several years. The results are shown in table 4.5.1.

In the years 1955–56 and subsequently, the mortality rate was lower and the symptoms of the disease less severe than in the first two years of testing. The same batch of virus was used each year, so the difference in mortality must be a result of the rabbits' evolving resistance.

The generation time of the rabbit is normally one year while that of the virus is a matter of hours. It is not surprising then, that the virus has quickly evolved increased

Table 4.5.1 *Severity of symptoms caused by one strain of myxoma virus over four years*

Year of capture of rabbits	Percentage of rabbits with symptoms		
	Severe and fatal	Moderate	Mild
1953	95	5	0
1954	93	5	2
1955	61	26	13
1956	75	14	11

adaptation to its new environment, the European rabbit. The character of greatest adaptive value in the virus is not its ability to kill its host but to spread. A virulent virus kills within two weeks of infection, during six days of which the rabbit can pass on the disease. A less virulent virus allows the rabbit to remain infective for 25 days. Mosquitoes do not bite dead rabbits. Consequently, when the host dies, so do all its viruses. The least virulent viruses do not kill the host at all but this is not necessarily to the advantage of the virus, because the host that recovers does so by destroying the viruses that infect it. An equilibrium point is reached where the virus keeps its host in an infectious state for as long as possible.

Myxomatosis was introduced accidentally into Britain in 1953 and only two years later had reduced the rabbit population by 90%. Here, myxomatosis is spread by the rabbit flea rather than by blood sucking mosquitoes. Fleas tend to stay on their host until it dies, when they then look for new hosts. A decline in the virulence of myxoma virus was not as noticeable in Britain as it was in Australia, where the rabbit flea is absent. In Britain, highly virulent virus strains were still present six years after introduction. Rabbits have been increasing since 1959 and are again widespread and abundant but outbreaks of

myxomatosis occur every now and then in localities where rabbit population density becomes high.

In Australia, rabbits are now controlled by poisoning with sodium monofluoroacetate, known as '1080'. In western Australia there are 33 species of leguminous plants which contain monofluoroacetate and which have been frequently responsible for poisoning domestic livestock. Animals such as the bush-tailed possum and the western grey kangaroo occur in association with these plants, can eat them without being poisoned and are resistant to '1080'. The same or similar species from other parts of Australia where monofluoro-acetate containing plants are absent, do not show resistance to this compound. Natural selection has brought about resistance in native animals; it must surely be only a matter of time before rabbits too evolve resistance to '1080'.

1 Why was the spread of myxomatosis more successful in the east of Australia than in the arid west?

2 Explain the difference between passive acquired immunity and genetically determined resistance to disease.

3 The data in table 4.5.1 indicate that wild rabbits were becoming genetically resistant to the standard myxoma virus. Suggest an alternative interpretation of the results.

4 In testing the rabbits for resistance, why is it necessary to use a standard strain of virus?

5 Explain how the short generation time of the virus can lead to rapid adaptation to its new host.

6 Explain how the habits of the virus vectors (flea and mosquito) can account for the maintenance of virulent virus strains in Britain but favour avirulence in Australia.

5   New techniques for gene manipulation

Introduction

In his book *A short history of genetics* (1965), L. C. Dunn said 'Distinctions between pure and applied, theoretical and practical have never been sharply drawn in genetics' yet at that time, one might have been forgiven for failing to see any practical value of over thirty years' research into the molecular genetics of bacteria and viruses. Pure research yields knowledge valuable in its own right and should not need the justification that it may prove to be of practical benefit in the future. Nevertheless, pure research in molecular biology has played a significant part in the 'biotechnological revolution'.

Biotechnology is the application to industry of biological processes. One such process, alcoholic fermentation, has been practised for over 8000 years. Other examples of old established food and drink biotechnology include the making of vinegar, yogurt, soy sauce, bean curd and cheese. Since the latter half of the nineteenth century when Louis Pasteur discovered that microorganisms were responsible for fermentation, bacteria and fungi have been set to work for us with ever increasing efficiency. Until recently, all organisms involved in biotechnology were adapted for their functions as a result of natural and artificial selection of intraspecific variation. A revolution came in the early 1970s with the discovery of enzymes which can be used to cut and join DNA so making it possible to change genotypes by unconventional routes. This is known as **recombinant DNA technology** and is largely responsible for the current surge of interest in biotechnology. An associated area of research is *in vitro* culture of plant and animal cells. *In vitro* means literally 'in glass' and is applied to events or processes that are made to happen outside the normal environment. The term which relates to processes or events in the living organism is *in vivo*.

Plant cell and tissue culture

If small pieces of plant tissue, called **explants**, are cultured *in vitro* in a medium containing nutrients and plant growth regulators, the cells will divide mitotically to produce an unorganised mass called a **callus**. By suitable adjustment of the growth regulators, the callus of some species can be induced to form small shoots which are capable of growth into mature plants (figure 5.1). Callus can be increased by subculture, i.e. cutting it into several pieces and placing them in separate dishes of culture medium.

An explant from meristematic tissue such as shoot tip, may develop plantlets directly without prior callus formation. Use of meristem or callus culture for rapid asexual cloning is called **micropropagation** and it is employed commercially for ornamental plants such as orchids, freesias and gladioli and for the production of virus-free plants, e.g. potatoes and strawberries. The method is particularly suitable for the propagation of adult forest trees in which selective breeding is made difficult due to the long life cycle, and for oil and date palms where conventional methods of vegetative propagation are not applicable.

Figure 5.1   *Callus with regenerating plantlets*

One of the problems with callus culture is that cells show high rates of spontaneous mutation, with the result that regenerated plants are not necessarily genetically identical. However, this increased variability, called **somaclonal variation**, is of potential value for artificial selection and has already been used in sugar cane improvement.

Many useful plant products such as codeine, quinine, caffeine and pyrethrum may act as deterrents to pests but are not essential for the plant's survival. These **secondary metabolites** are at present extracted from whole plants. Methods are now being developed for growing suspensions of cells, derived from callus, in large vats and then extracting secondary metabolites from them. In Japan the method has been successfully applied to production of the red pigment shikonin.

Anther culture is another example of *in vitro* plant tissue culture which has potential for the improvement of economically important plants. Immature pollen grains in an anther can be induced to undergo repeated mitotic divisions and give rise to haploid plants. The method has been successful in over a hundred species but there are many difficulties to be overcome such as, in grasses, a tendency to produce a high proportion of albino plants. Artificially doubling the chromosomes of haploids allows immediate production of completely homozygous plants. Anther culture with subsequent chromosome doubling has been used in the improvement of commercial rice varieties.

It is sometimes possible to obtain viable progeny by carrying out a **wide cross**, a conventional cross between two different species. The progeny may then be backcrossed to one or both of the parental species in order to transfer desirable genes (see exercise 2.2). In some wide crosses, fertilisation and embryo formation are successful but the embryo dies due to the endosperm's failure to nourish it properly. These embryos can sometimes be rescued through *in vitro* culture and raised into mature plants. This is called **embryo culture** and has been successful in crosses amongst various species of forage legumes (clover, *Trifolium* species).

Genetic engineering by cell hybridisation

In a sense, all deliberate manipulation of genotypes by conventional breeding methods can be described as genetic engineering but the term has come to mean the bringing together, in the same cell, of DNA from two different species of organism. In **eukaryotes** (organisms whose cells have a true nucleus, i.e. all animals, fungi and the higher plants) the conventional means of recombining DNA is by the process of sexual reproduction, but by this means DNA can be recombined normally only within the same species. However, new technology has made it possible to bypass the sexual process in order to bring about genetic recombination in somatic (i.e. non-sex) cells.

One way to recombine DNA is to cause somatic cells from two different species to fuse, a process analogous to the fusion of gametes in sexual reproduction. With plant cells, the cell membrane must first be exposed by incubating cells from a leaf or other tissue with cellulase and pectinase, enzymes which digest the cell walls. The naked cells are called **protoplasts** (figure 5.2) and must be maintained in a suitable osmotic environment to prevent their shrinking or bursting. Proto-

Figure 5.2   *(a) Protoplasts – plant cells isolated from their cell walls*

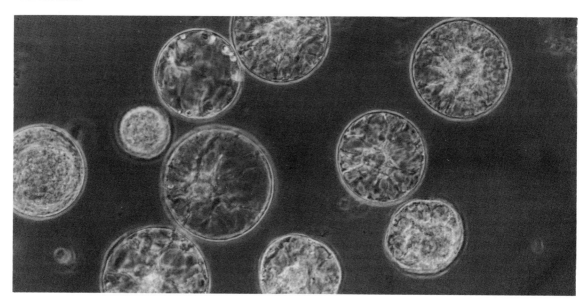

Figure 5.2   *(b) a–e successive stages in protoplast fusion*

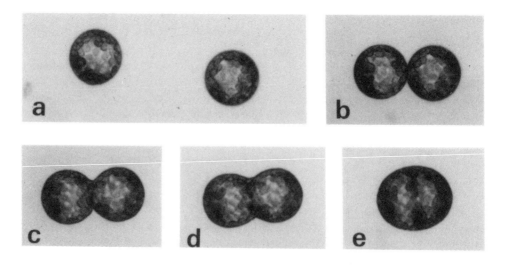

plasts can be induced to fuse by incorporating certain chemicals into the culture medium or by subjecting them to an electrical current. When the fused protoplasts are from different species the process is known as **somatic hybridisation**. It has been successful with species which are impossible to hybridise conventionally, like the tomato and potato. The cells soon start to divide and form a callus. A few species may be induced to regenerate whole plants but unfortunately, for cereals and most legumes, plant regeneration from protoplast culture has not proven possible. Somatic hybridisation could be used to create novel synthetic species but even where hybrid plants can be regenerated from the fused protoplasts they are unlikely to be fertile unless the parent species are closely related.

Protoplast fusion produces cells with hybrid cytoplasm, i.e. with organelles derived from two different sources, and by this means it may be possible to transfer cytoplasmically determined male sterility or herbicide resistance from one species or variety to another. (See exercises 2.8 and 3.3.)

Fusion of animal cells is utilised in the production of **monoclonal antibodies**. This is a development of *in vitro* gene manipulation which is of profound importance to scientific research. Antibodies are proteins which recognise and bind to other molecules. Each antibody binds to only one kind of molecule and this specificity can be exploited by investigators wanting to identify or label particular molecules but it has been difficult to obtain antibodies in a sufficiently pure form.

Antibodies are made by lymphocytes (white blood cells) in the spleen and by circulating plasma cells. Each lymphocyte secretes only one kind of antibody and so does the clone of plasma cells derived from it. The traditional way of obtaining antibodies against, say, a virus, is to inject an animal with the virus and isolate antibodies from its blood serum. But the virus stimulates the activity of several different lymphocytes so the isolated

'antibody' will be a mixture of several kinds, and the mixture varies from animal to animal.

Lymphocytes do not grow in culture but tumour cells do. In 1975 Cesar Milstein in Cambridge, England, succeeded in fusing tumour cells with spleen cells to make hybrid cells combining characteristics from both parental cell types; they produce antibody and readily proliferate in culture. A single hybrid cell gives rise to a clone of cells, all secreting the same antibody, i.e. a monoclonal antibody. Monoclonal antibodies are already used in diagnosis of disease, for blood grouping, for matching tissue types in organ transplant operations and for isolating proteins from a mixture.

The prime object of Milstein's research programme was to investigate the genetic control of antibodies, not to produce monoclonal antibodies, but here is an example of how the results of 'pure' research are finding applications in improving human health.

In cell fusion, chromosomes are brought together in novel combinations but the chromosomes themselves do not necessarily undergo any change in structure. In other techniques of *in vitro* gene manipulation, recombinant DNA molecules are constructed by joining together pieces of DNA from different sources and then introducing them into plant or animal cells or, more commonly, into bacteria. This aspect of genetic engineering is called recombinant DNA technology.

Principles of recombinant DNA technology using bacteria

The greatest progress in recombinant DNA work has been made with the most well-known of organisms genetically, *Escherichia coli*, a bacterium which lives naturally in the large intestine of humans and other mammals. In the laboratory it is easily grown in petri dishes of nutrient agar or in flasks of nutrient broth where it has a rapid reproductive rate. Genetic engineering of bacteria using recombinant DNA essentially involves

Figure 5.3 *Major steps in genetic engineering of bacteria using recombinant DNA*

Step 1. Obtain required DNA fragments.

There are three ways that this is commonly done:
(i) by digesting already existing DNA molecules with enzymes called **restriction endonucleases**;
(ii) by making a DNA complementary copy of messenger RNA for a known protein;
(iii) by making the required gene by joining together nucleotides *in vitro*.

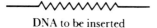

DNA to be inserted

Step 2. Join DNA fragments to a vector.

DNA fragments taken up by a cell will not replicate by themselves. They must be inserted into a piece of DNA that is capable of self-replication such as a naturally occurring circular DNA molecule called a **plasmid**. When a plasmid is used to replicate an inserted DNA fragment, it is called a **vector**. A vector with an inserted fragment is called a **recombinant DNA molecule**. Viruses that infect bacteria can also be used as vectors.

Plasmid containing inserted DNA

Step 3. Introduce recombinant DNA molecules into bacteria.

The gut bacteria *Escherichia coli* are usually used in these experiments. If bacteria and plasmids are mixed together in a test tube some of the bacteria will take up a plasmid and those that do are said to be **transformed**. The rate of transformation can be increased if viruses are used as vectors because these insert their DNA directly into the bacterial cell.

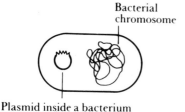

Plasmid inside a bacterium

Step 4. Find the bacteria which have taken up the correct piece of DNA.

It would be very difficult if not impossible to identify a single transformed bacterium so the bacteria are spread on to nutrient agar in a petri dish. The agar also contains a substance such as an antibiotic which allows growth of only transformed bacteria. By repeated cell division, each transformed bacterium gives rise to a visible spot called a **colony** made up of millions of identical copies of the original. A colony is therefore a **clone**. Any DNA which was taken up by the original bacterium has been copied over and over again, i.e. it has been cloned. **Gene cloning** is an alternative name for genetic engineering.

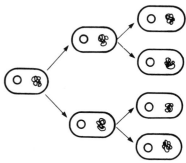

One transformed bacterium divides to form a clone of recombinant bacteria.

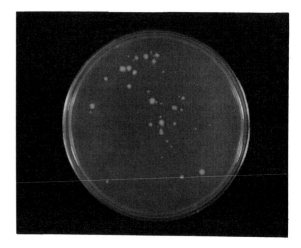

Colonies of bacteria on an agar plate. Some of these are clones of the required recombinant bacteria.

making new DNA molecules and inserting them into cells where they can replicate (multiply) as the cells multiply. Figure 5.3 explains the four major steps involved and some of the methods of achieving them. These are explained in greater detail in exercises 5.3 and 5.4.

Methods of DNA transfer between bacteria

In order to be able to understand the recombinant DNA techniques outlined in the following exercises, it is necessary to know something about natural processes of genetic recombination in bacteria. Bacteria are haploid, single celled organisms that reproduce asexually by binary fission. Their genetic material is a closed loop ('circle') of DNA and is called a chromosome but it is not associated with protein in the same way as in eukaryotes, nor is it enclosed within a nuclear envelope. Bacteria are **prokaryotes**. Elaborate mechanisms to ensure equal distribution of the hereditary material, mitosis and meiosis, are unnecessary because all the information is encoded in a single molecule. The DNA is attached to the cell membrane at or near the point where replication starts. After replication, the new molecule also becomes attached to the membrane and as the cell elongates prior to division, the two molecules are pulled apart. Although they are asexually reproducing, bacteria do possess mechanisms for acquiring and donating DNA. These mechanisms, **transformation**, **transduction** and **conjugation**, are very briefly described in this section. Further details may be found in general genetics books such as those given in the suggested reading list.

Transformation When cells die and disintegrate, DNA is released. Some species of bacteria are capable of taking up this DNA from their environment and integrating it into their own genome where it is able to replicate along with the rest of the chromosome. The

first evidence that genetic information could be transferred between bacteria came in 1928 with the experiments of Griffith who showed that non-virulent *Streptococcus pneumoniae* could be transformed into virulent bacteria if they were cultured in the presence of killed virulent bacteria. In 1944, Avery, MacLeod and McCarty identified the 'transforming principle' as DNA. The term transformation is now also used to describe the uptake of artificially constructed DNA by plant cells as well as by bacteria.

Transduction Bacteria are attacked by a number of viruses, called **bacteriophages** or simply **phages**, which are essentially a single molecule of nucleic acid (DNA or RNA) covered by a protein coat. A phage reproduces by inserting its own nucleic acid into a bacterium and directing the synthesis of new phage particles using the host cell's machinery. Normally the phages released from the host cell are exact replicas of the initial infecting virus but occasionally a piece of the host cell's DNA becomes packaged inside a virus coat. When such a virus infects a new host, bacterial DNA is transferred (transduced) and may become incorporated into the host's chromosome. Some genetic engineering experiments involve packaging the required DNA into virus coats in order to increase the chance of the DNA entering a host cell.

Conjugation Conjugation, unlike transformation or transduction, requires cell to cell contact through a tubular outgrowth of one of the cells called a sex pilus (figure 5.4). The genes which are responsible for controlling the production of a sex pilus are found not on the chromosome but on a **plasmid**. Plasmids are small circles of DNA found inside some bacteria in addition to the bacterial chromosome. There is enough DNA in a plasmid to code for several proteins together with a region called the origin of replication which enables the plasmid to make further copies of itself. The first plasmid to be discovered was

Figure 5.4 *Transmission electron micrograph of*
conjugating bacteria, one 'male' and two 'females'

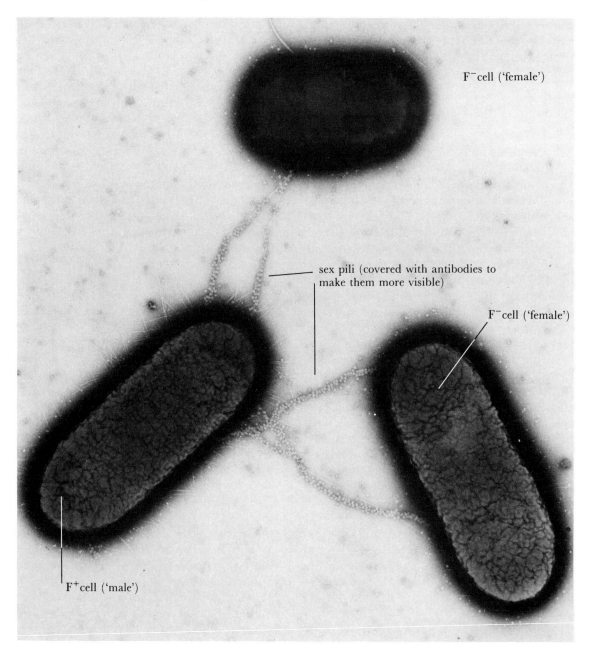

F⁻cell ('female')

sex pili (covered with antibodies to
make them more visible)

F⁻cell ('female')

F⁺cell ('male')

the F (fertility) factor or F plasmid. *E. coli*
containing F plasmids (F⁺ cells) can conju-
gate with cells lacking them (F⁻ cells). The F⁺
cell grows a sex pilus which makes a cytoplasmic bridge with an F⁻ cell. Then an enzyme
makes a break in the sugar-phosphate backbone in one of the DNA strands of the
plasmid. One end passes through the sex pilus

into the F⁻ cell and acts as a template for synthesis of a complementary strand. The F⁻ cell has been converted to F⁺. The single strand left behind in the F⁺ cell also synthesises a complementary strand and so retains a complete plasmid. Genes on the F plasmid not only code for proteins to make the sex pili but also for its own replication and transfer. Occasionally, bacterial chromosomal DNA becomes attached to the plasmid and in this way can be transferred to another bacterium. Some strains of *E. coli* (called Hfr strains) have a plasmid permanently attached to the chromosome and therefore show a high frequency of transfer of chromosomal genes.

Plasmids in nature

F is only one of many naturally occurring plasmids now known. They are all able to multiply in their host cell but not all can be transferred to other cells by conjugation. Non-conjugative plasmids are distributed to daughter cells at cell division. Plasmids are not regarded as additional chromosomes because they are dispensable, i.e. bacteria can function perfectly well without them. Most plasmids have come to the notice of investigators because they include genes that affect the phenotype of the host, such as resistance to antibiotics (exercise 5.1). Genes which confer on bacteria the ability to break down the herbicide 2,4-D and components of mineral oils or to fix nitrogen are also found on plasmids. The number of copies in each cell can vary from one or two to about 100, smaller plasmids generally having higher copy numbers.

Plasmids are particularly important as vectors in recombinant DNA work with bacteria because DNA can be inserted into them and will be replicated when the plasmid replicates. Parts of different plasmids can be cut out and joined together to construct new plasmids with desired properties.

Agrobacterium tumefaciens has been using plasmids for genetic engineering probably since long before *Homo sapiens* evolved. This bacterium is the causative agent of plant tumours called crown galls. It has been discovered that part of a plasmid (called the Ti, tumour inducing plasmid) passes from the infecting bacteria into the host plant cells. The plant cells are therefore said to have been transformed. The bacteria feed on unusual organic compounds called opines and the transferred DNA contains genes which bring about the synthesis of these compounds using the host cells' raw materials. It also alters the balance of growth factors in the plant, causing proliferation of the naturally genetically engineered cells into a tumour. In other words, *Agrobacterium tumefaciens* (literally 'tumour causing field bacterium') is cloning its own food supply.

Genetic engineering of higher organisms

In recent years it has become possible to exploit the natural genetic engineering capabilities of *Agrobacterium tumefaciens* in the transformation of higher plants. In nature, the bacteria respond to chemical signals released by wounded plants, attach themselves to a cell and transfer into the plant cell a portion of the Ti plasmid, called T-DNA, by a process very similar to conjugation. T-DNA is a vector of the genes for opine production and tumour formation. It integrates into a chromosome and so is replicated and inherited by subsequent cell generations. It also contains the correct signals for its genes to be 'switched on' in the plant cell. It has not proved too difficult to engineer the T-DNA to suit our own purposes. At present, methods for gene transfer are being tested by inserting marker genes whose effects are easily detectable, such as antibiotic resistance. However, if the techniques can be perfected, it may be possible to transform crop plants with genes controlling valuable production traits.

The aim of this kind of work, then, is to produce plants containing genes from other species, so-called **transgenic** plants; but inserting DNA into plant cells is only part of the problem. It is also necessary to grow complete plants from the transformed cells. In species susceptible to *Agrobacterium* infection, transgenic plants have been raised from pieces of infected leaf and root tissue. Protoplasts can be transformed by several methods but cereals unfortunately do not readily regenerate from protoplasts. However, a recent report describes a method of producing transgenic cereals avoiding all the problems of tissue culture. DNA injected into the cells of developing flowers of rye plants brought about the transformation of a small proportion of gametes. By normal fertilisation and development, these gametes gave rise to transgenic plants in the next generation.

With animals, only the zygote and the first few cells derived from it can develop into a complete organism. Transgenic mice have been produced by injecting fertilised eggs with DNA containing the gene for rat growth hormone. This DNA was incorporated into a chromosome in some of the embryos which subsequently grew into adults of almost twice normal size. Furthermore, the inserted gene was present in the germ line of these animals and was transmitted to their progeny. Such work is encouraging for similar experiments with farm animals. It shows that the *in vitro* transfer of animal genes can be done. However, it is not without difficulties. For instance, when introduced DNA integrates into a chromosome, it may insert into another gene and destroy that gene's function. Secondly, little is known about how genes are controlled in different tissues so even if a gene can be transferred, there is no guarantee that it will function normally in the appropriate tissue.

All genetic engineering of higher plants and animals is as yet in the experimental stage. The new technology has opened up exciting avenues for the improvement of domesticated species but it is likely to supplement rather than replace conventional methods of genetic engineering by sexual recombination and selection.

Conclusion

Public interest in biotechnology is largely a result of the recent contributions from recombinant DNA research. In many applications of this work, what is required is the protein product of a cloned gene, such as an enzyme or a hormone, but success in obtaining the product in sufficient quantities demands a detailed knowledge of gene structure and function. The greatest impact of recombinant DNA technology so far is here, in the study of genes themselves. Industrial, medical and agricultural applications are coming but rather more slowly than at first anticipated.

5.1 Drug resistance in bacteria

Just as pests evolve resistance to pesticides (chapter 3) so bacteria evolve resistance to antimicrobial drugs and the search for new drugs must go on. The antibiotic penicillin has been widely used for more than forty years and with such long continued selection pressure it is not surprising to find that some pathogenic bacteria are now completely resistant.

When antibiotic resistant bacteria were discovered soon after introduction of the drugs in the 1940s, there were two conflicting views as to how resistance arises:

Hypothesis 1   Most bacterial cells adapt to their new environment by adjusting their enzyme activity.

Hypothesis 2   The drug kills or prevents the growth of most cells but some show spontaneous mutation to a form which is able to grow and divide in the presence of the drug.

In the early 1950s Lederberg and Lederberg developed the technique of **replica-plating** and obtained results supporting one of these hypotheses (figure 5.1.1).

1   Do the results of the experiment shown in figure 5.1.1 support hypothesis 1 or hypothesis 2?

Figure 5.1.1 *A replica-plating experiment*

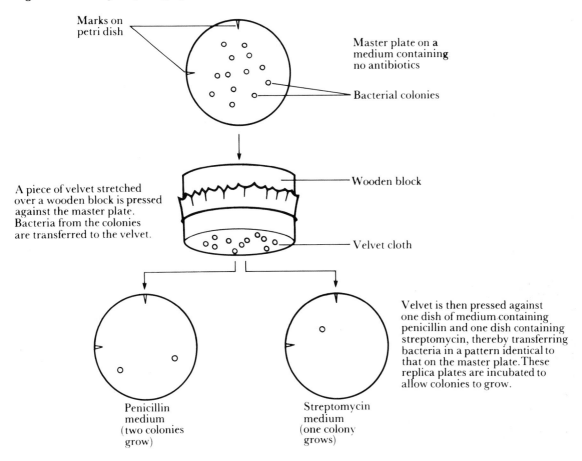

Marks on petri dish

Master plate on a medium containing no antibiotics

Bacterial colonies

A piece of velvet stretched over a wooden block is pressed against the master plate. Bacteria from the colonies are transferred to the velvet.

Wooden block

Velvet cloth

Velvet is then pressed against one dish of medium containing penicillin and one dish containing streptomycin, thereby transferring bacteria in a pattern identical to that on the master plate. These replica plates are incubated to allow colonies to grow.

Penicillin medium (two colonies grow)

Streptomycin medium (one colony grows)

2 What results might have been expected if the alternative hypothesis were true?

3 Why were the replica plates marked in the same position, relative to the colonies, as the original plate?

4 If the original plate were replica-plated on to a medium containing both streptomycin and penicillin, what results would you expect?

5 Mutation of a chromosomal gene resulting in resistance to one antibiotic is expected about once in 10^7 cell divisions.
   (a) What is the probability that a cell would acquire, by mutation, resistance to two antibiotics simultaneously?
   (b) Some chronic bacterial diseases such as tuberculosis are treated with combinations of two or more drugs. How does this reduce the chance of resistance developing?
   (c) Under ideal conditions bacteria such as *E. coli* can reproduce every 20 minutes. How long would it take for one cell to give rise to a clone of at least 10^7 cells?

Bacteria in nature are rarely living under ideal conditions. If *E. coli* reproduced at this rate in the human gut we would be excreting many kilograms of them every few hours!

Because bacteria are haploid organisms, every gene counts, i.e. they cannot maintain potentially valuable genes in a recessive state.

If a gene mutates to give resistance to an antibiotic then the gene's original function will be impaired and the bacteria possessing it grow slowly compared with susceptible bacteria in an antibiotic-free environment (see also exercise 3.5). Therefore in the absence of antibiotic the gene for resistance will be selectively eliminated from the population. Resistance to antibiotics should not be a serious problem, but it is.

In the early 1960s Japanese microbiologists discovered that neither of the hypotheses above was correct but that genes for resistance to antimicrobial drugs were found on plasmids, now called **R plasmids**. Two biologically important features of R plasmids are that they can carry several resistance genes, so conferring multiple resistance on their bacterial host, and that they can be transferred by conjugation not only between members of the same species but also across species boundaries. Thus resistance can be passed 'horizontally' as well as by the more familiar 'vertical' route from parent to progeny (figure 5.1.2).

Bacteria with R plasmids do not have to sacrifice the normal function of a chromosomal gene to attain resistance but plasmids do represent a burden on the host cell in the energy and resources they consume for replication. Even so, R plasmids are not readily eliminated in the absence of antibiotics because they are continually transferred horizontally to cells without them. The plasmids are able to acquire additional resistance genes such that some now confer resistance to seven or eight antimicrobial drugs. Exposure to only one of them will create selection pressure in favour of the plasmid as a whole. Because of **multiple resistance** some bacterial diseases are becoming almost untreatable and the problem is acute where the drugs are most commonly in use, in developing countries, hospitals and agriculture.

In many developing countries antibiotics can be bought over the counter without a doctor's prescription and so are used widely and indiscriminately. Frequent exposure to antibiotics of harmless gut-dwelling bacteria such as *E. coli* creates selection pressure for R plasmids with the risk that they can be transferred by conjugation to species of pathogenic bacteria. This was apparently the

Figure 5.1.2 *Vertical and horizontal transfer of plasmid-borne drug resistance*

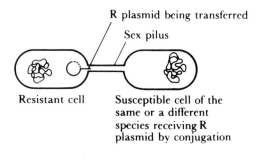

Vertical transmission

Bacterial chromosome

R plasmid

Resistant parent cell

Resistant progeny

Horizontal transmission

R plasmid being transferred

Sex pilus

Resistant cell

Susceptible cell of the same or a different species receiving R plasmid by conjugation

cause of an epidemic of typhoid fever in Mexico in 1972–73. The first choice drug, chloramphenicol, as well as streptomycin, sulphonamides and tetracycline all proved useless and there were many fatalities before effective treatment was found in ampicillin.

Intense selection pressure for R plasmids also occurs in hospitals where antibiotics are widely used both for treatment and prevention of infection. An increase in the occurrence of multiple resistance emphasises the importance of hygienic practice because one cannot be certain of an easy cure for hospital acquired infections.

In intensive beef production, calves are kept under conditions which favour the spread of infections such as enteritis caused by *Salmonella*. Calves therefore receive frequent doses of antibiotics to treat and prevent disease. Low doses of antibiotics have been found to promote growth in animals and so are also routinely incorporated into their food.

Bacteria from the guts of slaughtered animals regularly contaminate the meat and are passed on to the next step in the food chain, us. Ingestion of *Salmonella* on undercooked meat causes food poisoning and since about 1963 *Salmonella* has become resistant to more and more antibiotics. In 1979 a strain appeared which is resistant to seven antimicrobial drugs.

The proportion of antibiotic resistant *E. coli* in the alimentary canal of calves is often as high as 60% compared with 0.02% in humans. These non-pathogenic bacteria are also transmitted from animals to humans on contaminated meat and are able to persist in the human gut for about ten days.

6 Epidemics caused by multiply resistant pathogens such as the typhoid epidemic in Mexico have shown that harmless bacteria which are constantly exposed to antibiotics can pose a threat to human health. How?

7 Explain why the proportion of antibiotic resistant *E. coli* in the gut of calves is so much higher than in humans.

8 In 1969 a UK government committee recommended that drugs which are useful for treating human disease should not be used as growth promoters in animal feedstuffs. Similar precautions are now taken in other European countries. Explain the reasoning behind this recommendation.

5.2 *Protein synthesis*

Industrial applications of recombinant DNA technology require that the gene inserted into bacteria or other organisms should function in its new location. Cutting and joining DNA and inserting it into bacteria is now a matter of routine but getting the gene to work is not so simple. There is much we still need to know, but the technology itself is allowing very rapid progress in the study of genes and their functions. This exercise provides revision of the principles of protein synthesis and introduces some details which you need for an understanding of recombinant DNA methods. Protein synthesis occurs in two stages which may be summarised as follows.

$$\text{DNA} \xrightarrow{\text{transcription}} \text{RNA} \xrightarrow{\text{translation}} \text{Protein}$$

Transcription

1 Write a few sentences to describe the process of transcription. Use as many of the following words as you can; template, complementary, ribonucleotides, hydrogen bonds, messenger RNA.

2 Figure 5.2.1 shows an mRNA strand being synthesised on a DNA template. Name bases 1, 2, 3, 4 and 5 in the diagram.

3 What is the name of the enzyme mentioned in figure 5.2.1?

If you understand the process of transcription, you may have asked yourself questions such as: 'Can transcription proceed in both directions along a single strand of DNA? Can both strands of DNA be transcribed? Why does transcription start in a particular place on the DNA? What stops transcription?' Answers to these questions are required if DNA is to be successfully manipulated.

Transcription always occurs in one direction relative to the DNA template because of the way that the nucleotides are added to a growing chain (see figure 5.2.1). Single strands of DNA and RNA have a definite orientation, with a phosphate group at one end, the 5′ (five prime) end and a free OH group on carbon atom 3 of the sugar at the other, the 3′ end. In double stranded molecules, the two strands run in opposite directions.

Not all DNA codes for protein, probably less than 50% of it does in humans; so what about the rest? Some codes for ribosomal and transfer RNA and some exerts control over transcription but the function of much of the DNA in human cells is unknown.

Figure 5.2.1 *Synthesis of mRNA on a DNA template*

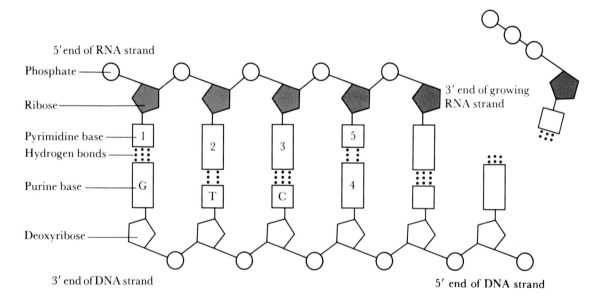

Incoming ribonucleoside triphosphate. Two phosphate groups are removed as the 5′ end of the nucleotide joins the 3′ end of the RNA strand. This provides the energy for an enzyme (see question 3) to extend the sugar phosphate backbone.

Transcription of a protein coding sequence into RNA is brought about by **RNA polymerase**. This enzyme recognises and binds to a specific sequence of bases on the DNA called a **promoter** which occurs before or 'upstream' of the protein coding sequence. As the enzyme moves downstream from the promoter, it causes the two DNA strands to move apart and an mRNA strand to be built up in the 5′ to 3′ direction. Promoters occur on either of the two DNA strands in a double helix, so the strand which is transcribed is not the same one for every gene. Every protein coding sequence does not necessarily have its own promoter so it is possible for a single mRNA strand to carry information for two or more proteins. The signal to stop transcribing is thought to be a sequence of bases which causes the growing mRNA chain to fold up in a certain way.

Translation

Translation is the conversion of the message in mRNA into a polypeptide. In prokaryotes, where there is no nuclear membrane, translation of an mRNA strand begins while it is still being synthesised. In eukaryotes the mRNA has to be 'edited' before it leaves the nucleus.

Protein coding sequences in eukaryotic genes are seldom continuous but are broken up by sequences of bases which do not code for protein. They are described as 'split genes' and the non-coding sequences are called **introns** (figure 5.2.2). The function of these introns is not known but their mRNA transcripts are cut out by enzymes before translation. Translation of the edited mRNA then proceeds in a similar manner to translation in prokaryotes.

Figure 5.2.2 *Transcription and editing of a split gene*

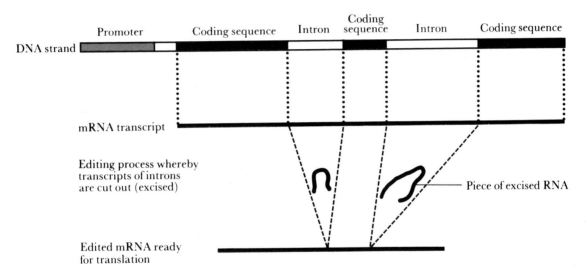

4 Rearrange the following sentences in the correct order to form a logical account of translation in prokaryotes.

A   The tRNA with the anticodon to AUG forms hydrogen bonds with the complementary codon on mRNA and brings the amino acid methionine into position on the ribosome.

B   The ribosome moves along the mRNA until the codon AUG is aligned in the appropriate position.

C   The signal to start translation is the codon AUG.

D   The ribosome moves along to the next codon and the first tRNA is released.

E   On one loop of the molecule is a group of three unpaired bases called an anticodon.

F   Near the 5′ end of the mRNA is a sequence of bases called the **ribosome binding site** which enables it to attach to a ribosome.

G   There are at least twenty different kinds, each one chemically linked to a particular amino acid.

H   The polypeptide is released from the ribosome.

I   Amino acids are added one by one to the growing chain until the ribosome reaches one of the termination codons

UAA, UGA or UAG.

J   The next codon binds with the appropriate tRNA and a peptide bond is formed between the amino acids brought adjacent to each other on the ribosome.

K   In the cytoplasm are molecules of tRNA, short single strands which are folded and held in shape by hydrogen bonds between complementary bases.

5 The mRNA triplet AUG is the translation start signal and also the codon for methionine.
(a) What is the complementary triplet on the DNA?
(b) What is the corresponding anticodon on tRNA?

6 In your answer to question 4 about translation, underline any reference to base pairing.

7 Why is base pairing important in
(a) DNA replication; (b) transcription?

8 What do you understand by the 'genetic code'?

9 The following are all sequences of bases: anticodon, codon, intron, promoter, ribosome binding site.
(a) Which of them occur in RNA and which in DNA?
(b) Give a short definition of each one.

All prokaryotes and eukaryotes employ the same genetic code and for this reason it is described as a **universal code**. This means that a human or mouse gene which has been inserted into a bacterium should be able to function using the molecular machinery of the prokaryotic cell.

However, all is not as straightforward as at first appears. In genetic engineering experiments it has to be DNA not RNA which is introduced into bacteria because mRNA is broken up by enzymes after a few minutes. DNA is used because it is self-replicating and provides a permanent template for mRNA synthesis. Even when DNA has been successfully inserted into bacteria it does not necessarily yield a protein product which can be extracted from the cells. Some of the reasons are given below.

(1) The number of bases on the mRNA between the ribosome binding site and the start codon AUG is critical and is not the same for every gene, whether prokaryote or eukaryote. The wrong number of bases results in inefficiency of translation.

(2) The eukaryote promoter is not always recognised by the bacterial RNA polymerase so transcription is inefficient.

(3) Many newly synthesised proteins are non-functional until they have undergone some modification. For instance, human insulin has 58 fewer amino acids than the polypeptide from which it is derived, called preproinsulin. The 'insulin gene' in fact codes for preproinsulin which in the human pancreas is modified by the removal of two groups of amino acids to form functional insulin. The enzymes necessary to carry out this editing are not present in *E. coli*.

(4) Proteases in the bacterial cell are able to recognise foreign polypeptides and destroy them almost as soon as they are made.

(5) The eukaryote coding sequence is interrupted by introns and bacteria do not have the machinery for editing mRNA. If the unedited mRNA transcript is translated, the result will be a nonsense polypeptide.

If the object of an experiment is to clone a gene in order to study its base sequence then these problems are irrelevant. But if the protein product is required, the DNA must be inserted in such a way as to ensure efficient transcription, translation and where necessary, post-translational modification.

10 The conversion of information in DNA into a functioning protein involves a sequence of steps as shown in figure 5.2.3. Each of the reasons numbered before refers to a break in the sequence of steps, shown as a break in an arrow on the figure.

Copy the figure, then consider each reason given and put the number of that reason in the most appropriate box in the figure.

Figure 5.2.3

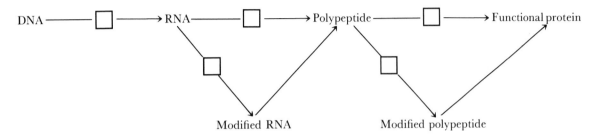

5.3 Recombinant DNA methods I. Cutting and joining DNA

An aim of recombinant DNA work with *E. coli* is to insert DNA from another species in such a way that it will be copied over and over again as the cells divide. The four major steps, outlined in the introduction, are:

(1) obtain the required DNA fragments;
(2) join DNA fragments to a vector;
(3) introduce recombinant DNA molecules into bacteria;
(4) find the bacteria which have taken up the correct piece of DNA.

This and the following exercise outline only a few of many techniques, in order to illustrate the principles of gene cloning. The present exercise concentrates on steps 1 and 2 above and exercise 5.4 describes steps 3 and 4. You will be carrying out an imaginary experiment to put the gene for human growth hormone into *E. coli*. The materials you require are:

(i) plasmids (to act as vectors);
(ii) cutting enzymes (to open up the circular plasmid and to cut the human DNA);
(iii) joining enzymes (to stick the inserted DNA into the vector);

(iv) human growth hormone genes.

It is fairly straightforward to isolate plasmid DNA from bacteria by centrifugation, and cutting and joining enzymes are available commercially; but how do we get human growth hormone genes? All we know is that the gene is somewhere in the human genome. (A **genome** is one complete set of chromosomes, i.e. a haploid set, but the word is sometimes used to describe all the chromosomes in a cell. The terms **haploid genome** and **diploid genome** make clear how the word is being used.)

The first step in obtaining the genes involves gently grinding up human cells to release the contents and then purifying the DNA. The resulting viscous fluid will contain many copies of the required gene together with every other gene in the genome. No further progress can be made until the DNA is chopped up into manageable pieces and then it will be possible to look for the piece that contains the required gene.

It was the discovery of DNA cutting enzymes in the early 1970s that gave the lead to recombinant DNA work. These enzymes, called **restriction endonucleases**, do not cut DNA at random but recognise particular sequences of bases. About 300 such enzymes are now known; some of the most useful recognise a sequence of six bases and cut within that region in such a way that they leave single stranded 'sticky ends' (table 5.3.1).

Table 5.3.1 *Some restriction endonucleases and their recognition sequences*

Name of enzyme	Recognition sequence	Sticky ends produced	
Bam HI	...G▼G A T C C... ...C C T A G▲G...	...G ...C C T A G	G A T C C... G...
Eco RI	...G▼A A T T C... ...C T T A A▲G...	...G ...C T T A A	A A T T C... G...
Hind III	...A▼A G C T T... ...T T C G A▲A...	...A ...T T C G A	A G C T T... A...

The arrows in the recognition sequences show where the enzyme cuts.

1 Look carefully at the recognition sequences of the enzymes in table 5.3.1. You should be able to see a pattern in each one. Use this pattern to complete the recognition sequences of the following restriction endonucleases.

Name of enzyme	Recognition sequence
Pst I	...C T G ? ? ?... ...G A C ? ? ?...
Sst I	...G A G ? ? ?... ...C T C ? ? ?...
Kpn I	...G G T ? ? ?... ...C C A ? ? ?...

2 A restriction enzyme recognising a six base-pair (bp) sequence cuts, on average, every $4^6 = 4096$ bp. One thousand base-pairs are known as one kilobase (kb). The human haploid genome is about 2.8×10^6 kb. If *Bam* HI cuts approximately every 4 kb, into approximately how many pieces does this enzyme cut the human haploid genome?

The gene we are looking for, the one for growth hormone, is somewhere on one of these pieces, assuming that it has not been cut in two as a result of having a *Bam* HI recognition site. The plasmid vector we shall use is called **pBR322** and is about 4.4 kb in circumference.

Figure 5.3.1 is a map of pBR322 showing the position of the recognition sites for three restriction enzymes (*Pst* I, *Eco* RI and *Bam* HI), the point of origin of DNA replication (*ori*) and two genes for resistance to the antibiotics ampicillin (*amp^R*) and tetracycline (*tet^R*). At 4.4 kb, pBR322 is approximately the same as the average length of one of the fragments of the human genome.

You are now ready to start your recombinant DNA experiment.

Figure 5.3.1 *Map of the plasmid pBR322*

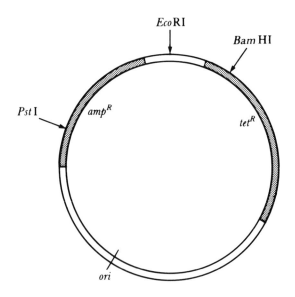

A Obtaining plasmids

To obtain your supply of plasmids, take a piece of lined A4 paper and divide it length-wise into 10 strips each 2 cm wide. Mark each strip as in figure 5.3.2. The shaded regions represent the genes for antibiotic resistance. A *Bam* HI recognition sequence is found within the *tet^R* gene. Write one base pair in one space made by the lines printed on the paper (this is not to scale of course). Cut out the strips of paper and stick the two ends of each one together to make a circular 'plasmid', pBR322.

B Obtaining human DNA fragments by cutting with a restriction endonuclease

We have used *Bam* HI to cut our purified human DNA (question 2) so if we were going to do this experiment authentically, we would need about 700 000 strips of paper to represent the fragments of human DNA, one of which includes the gene we want. We will use just ten fragments. Divide another piece of lined A4 paper lengthwise into 2 cm strips and cut them out. Mark the ends of each strip as in figure 5.3.3 and, with scissors (your '*Bam* HI

restriction endonuclease'), cut away the pieces indicated to leave 'single stranded sticky ends'. Number the strips 1 to 10 and on any one shade a region to represent the gene for growth hormone.

C Obtaining recombinant DNA molecules

For the time being, keep the human DNA fragments separate from the plasmids. With your '*Bam* HI endonuclease', cut the plasmids in the appropriate way (see table 5.3.1) in the recognition sequences but leave two of them uncut. Now mix together the plasmids and human DNA fragments. Because we have used the same restriction enzyme, the plasmids and human DNA have the same single stranded ends. When two such ends come near each other in the mixture, hydrogen bonds form between complementary bases and the ends stick together or **anneal**. Annealing does not require the intervention of an enzyme, but the hydrogen bonds are not permanent. An enzyme called **DNA ligase** is added to **ligate** annealed fragments by sealing the two gaps in the sugar–phosphate backbones (figure 5.3.4).

Figure 5.3.2

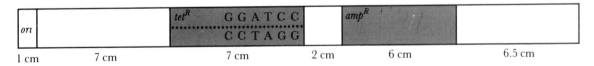

Figure 5.3.3

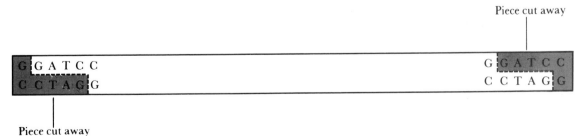

Figure 5.3.4 *The action of DNA ligase*

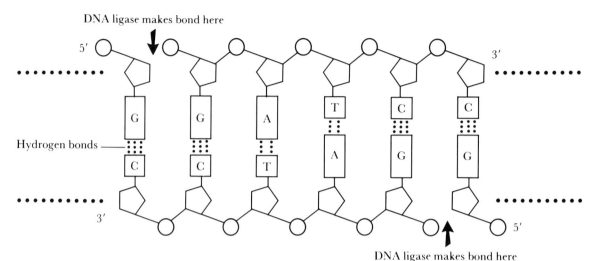

First anneal any two single stranded ends by fitting them together with complementary bases opposite. Then ligate them by fixing them with sticky tape ('DNA ligase'). Do the same with any other two ends. If you do this randomly, you will find that you have recircularised plasmids, circularised human DNA fragments, two or more human DNA fragments joined together, one or more human DNA fragments joined to a plasmid, two or more plasmids joined together (plasmid dimers) and some fragments which have not ligated at all. This is just what is found in the real experiment although modifications are employed to prevent plasmid recircularisation and dimer formation. Therefore if you have any of these, open them again into linear (open ended) fragments. The modifications in the procedure increase the chance of getting the required recombinant DNA molecules, i.e. one plasmid containing one inserted fragment (figure 5.3.5). Ensure that you have a number of recombinant plasmids as well as the two plasmids which were not attacked by the restriction endonuclease. Remember that we had 700 000 different fragments of human DNA. Of all the recombinant plasmids formed, on average only one in 700 000 will contain the gene we want. Retain all your strips of paper for exercise 5.4. They can be folded for easy storage.

In the experiment described in the present exercise, the whole of an organism's DNA is cut up with a restriction endonuclease and the fragments are allowed to recombine with plasmid DNA cut up with the same enzyme. Such a procedure is called a 'shotgun' experiment because, like a shotgun, it lacks precision, but since the position of the target (the required gene) is not known, the method will probably find it. The great majority of plasmids with inserted DNA will not carry the required fragment but nevertheless may be useful for another investigation, so once they have been cloned (see exercise 5.4) they are not discarded. The whole of the human genome can be maintained in 700 000 clones of bacteria and such a collection is called a **gene library**. In fact, gene libraries are constructed using vectors which can carry larger pieces of DNA than can a plasmid. Even so, the number of clones required to maintain a human gene library is in the region of 2.5×10^5 to 5.5×10^5.

A more precise alternative to the shotgun approach is to synthesise the gene *de novo* (i.e.

from scratch), a method that is suitable only if the protein product of the gene is known. One of the first genes to be artificially synthesised (in 1977) was that for somatostatin, a hormone of fourteen amino acids which has an effect antagonistic to human growth hormone. Because the amino acid sequence was known, the sequence of DNA bases coding for the protein could be worked out. Methods are available for stringing together nucleotides in a desired order; in fact it is now possible to purchase microcomputer controlled machines for making genes.

While a gene may be present only twice in a diploid cell, the mRNA transcript may be present in thousands of copies. Any cell transcribes only a small proportion of all the genes it contains; the human growth hormone gene for instance will be transcribed in cells of the pituitary gland. The total mRNA of a tissue can be purified and then an enzyme called **reverse transcriptase** can be used to make a DNA transcript of it. This enzyme is isolated from certain viruses and is so called because it carries out transcription in the

reverse direction from normal, making a single stranded DNA transcript (copy or **cDNA**) from an RNA template. Another enzyme is then used to make the DNA double stranded. We will still finish up with a lot of different pieces of DNA, corresponding to the number of types of mRNA in the tissue, but the number will be small compared to the 700 000 or so obtained from cutting total DNA. There is no danger with this method that the gene of interest will be cut in two by a restriction enzyme and a further advantage is that a cDNA gene contains no introns, making it more similar to a prokaryote gene. A minor disadvantage, the lack of sticky ends, is easily rectified by adding adenine nucleotides to the 3′ ends; the vector to be used is then provided with complementary thymine sticky ends.

3 This exercise has introduced three kinds of enzymes used in recombinant DNA work. State what they are and what they do.

5.4 Recombinant DNA methods II. Transformation and selection

This exercise makes use of the strips of paper resulting from exercise 5.3. If you have not already done so, fold each strip and circle into a manageable size. If any of them consist of three or more strips stuck together, put them on one side but do not discard anything at this stage. The paper strips represent the different kinds of DNA molecules which are now ready to be mixed with a liquid culture (suspension) of bacteria.

E. coli cells do not readily take up DNA from their environment but efficiency can be improved to 1% of cells by prior treatment with calcium chloride. Even then, only about 0.01% of the DNA pieces are taken into cells. Large fragments are less easily taken up so discard any paper strips or circles which consist of three or more pieces. The remainder

Figure 5.3.5 *Required recombinant DNA molecule*

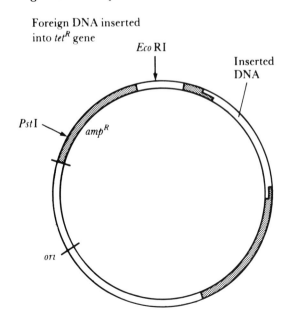

Foreign DNA inserted
into *tet*^{R} gene

represent the fragments which can successfully enter a cell.

A Transforming E. coli

For this part of the experiment you need fifteen petri dishes, to represent *E. coli* cells. Take one dish, representing one cell in 100, and put a DNA fragment inside it. The cell is now said to be **transformed**. In a similar way transform the remaining cells until you run out of either DNA fragments or cells. Spread out all fifteen dishes on a bench.

B Selecting transformed cells

Only some of the DNA that has entered a cell will be able to replicate. Inspect each piece of DNA and discard it
(a) if it is a linear fragment (i.e. not a circle) because DNA digesting enzymes in the bacteria destroy linear but not circular fragments.
(b) if it does not include *ori* because fragments lacking an origin of replication are not able to multiply.
Neither of these kinds of DNA will be inherited by the progeny of these transformed cells, so discard the paper strips but leave the empty dishes in position. All the remaining cells contain either a plasmid with an origin of replication or no plasmid at all (i.e. untransformed cells). Make sure that your collection of fifteen petri dishes includes some of both types. These are now cultured on an agar medium containing ampicillin where only cells containing the *amp*^{R} gene will survive and grow, forming colonies on an agar plate. Remove any 'cells' which do not contain *amp*^{R}.

This part of the procedure has left transformed cells only and each transformed cell contains a plasmid with the *amp*^{R} gene. In the real experiment you would now have a number of plates containing nutrient agar with ampicillin on which are growing colonies of bacteria. All of the bacteria in one colony contain identical copies of the plasmid that was taken up by the original cell from which that colony grew. In other words, the plasmid

has been cloned. But the different colonies contain different plasmids.

Make another copy of each of the petri dishes now in front of you. Ensure that you make an exact replica of the paper strip. Place the replica petri dish on top of the original. Each pair represents a bacterial colony, so arrange the pairs in a random manner as if they were distributed on an agar surface (see figure 5.3).

Most of your cells will contain recombinant plasmids because, in mixing plasmids with human DNA fragments, conditions were adjusted to encourage the formation of recombinant molecules. But there will be a number of non-recombinant plasmids, because they escaped either the restriction enzyme or the treatment to prevent rejoining of the cut ends.

C Selecting cells with recombinant plasmids

Each pair of identical petri dishes represents a bacterial colony growing on agar containing ampicillin. We want to isolate the colonies containing recombinant plasmids. To do this, we replica-plate (see exercise 5.1) on to a plate of agar containing tetracycline. Take one dish from each pair and arrange them on another part of the bench in exactly the same pattern as the remaining dishes. This is your replica-plate on tetracycline medium. Only those cells with an intact *tet*^{R} gene are resistant to tetracycline and are therefore able to grow. A piece of DNA inserted into the *tet*^{R} gene destroys its function. This is known as **insertional inactivation**. Inspect the plasmids on the tetracycline plate and take away any dish which does not contain an intact *tet*^{R} gene. Although tetracycline prevents growth of the cells we want, we are now able to identify on the master plate colonies containing recombinant plasmids.

D Selecting a particular clone

In a shotgun experiment like this one, we would hope at this stage to have 700 000 or so clones each containing one human DNA fragment. But because of the random nature of the approach, some fragments may be represented in more than one clone and others will not be represented at all. The next task is to find the clone or clones which contain the gene of interest. If we know enough about the gene to make part of it (see exercise 5.3) we can exploit the base pairing properties of nucleic acids to find the required clone.

Recombinant bacteria (those containing recombinant plasmids) are plated out on to fresh agar and allowed to form colonies. A replica is then transferred to nitrocellulose paper which is treated to remove everything

Figure 5.4.1 *Using a gene probe for identifying bacterial colonies carrying the required gene*

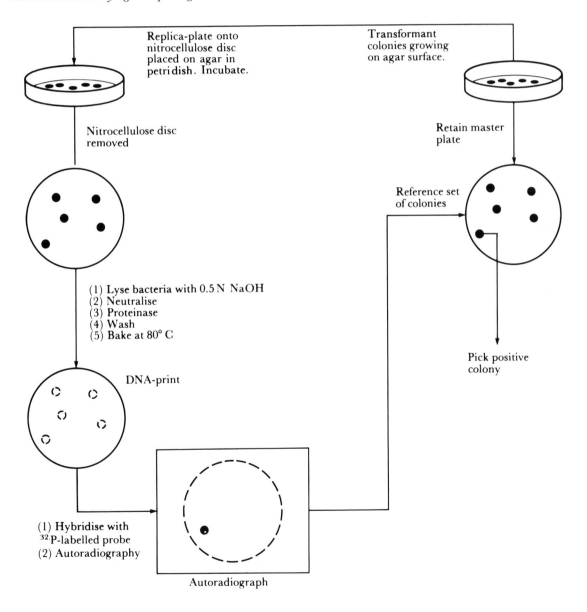

Replica-plate onto nitrocellulose disc placed on agar in petri dish. Incubate.

Transformant colonies growing on agar surface.

Nitrocellulose disc removed

Retain master plate

Reference set of colonies

(1) Lyse bacteria with 0.5 N NaOH
(2) Neutralise
(3) Proteinase
(4) Wash
(5) Bake at 80° C

Pick positive colony

DNA-print

(1) Hybridise with ^{32}P-labelled probe
(2) Autoradiography

Autoradiograph

except the DNA which is left tightly bound to the paper in its original position. The treatment also causes the double strands to separate at the hydrogen bonds.

The required gene in our experiment is that for growth hormone whose amino acid sequence is known. A radioactive **gene probe** can be made by joining together radioactively labelled nucleotides in the order corresponding to the protein's amino acid sequence.

1 Human growth hormone is a protein of 191 amino acids. How many DNA base pairs make up the coding region of this gene?

2 The actual gene may be longer than this. Why?

3 Knowledge of an amino acid sequence does not necessarily mean that its DNA coding sequence can be accurately predicted. Why not?

It is not necessary to make the whole of the sequence; a probe 15–20 nucleotides long is adequate. Another way of making a probe is to make a cDNA copy of purified mRNA transcripts of the gene (see exercise 5.3). A solution containing the single stranded radioactive probe is washed over the nitrocellulose paper and where it meets a complementary sequence, the probe will bind. This is called **hybridisation**. The more hydrogen bonds that form, the tighter the hybridisation and therefore long and/or exactly complementary probes are desirable. The paper is then washed to remove unbound probe, dried and autoradiographed. Dark spots on the autoradiograph reveal the presence of the probe and matching the pattern of the spots to the master plate locates the bacterial colonies carrying the required DNA. The procedure is illustrated in figure 5.4.1.

An alternative method is to find which colonies are manufacturing the required protein, using radioactively labelled monoclonal antibodies to the protein in question. However, gene expression (protein production) will only be efficient if the plasmid or virus

Figure 5.4.2 Sequence of steps involved in cloning DNA

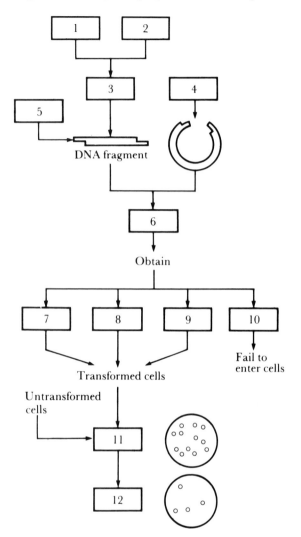

vectors have been specially engineered.

Some applications of recombinant DNA technology are described in exercise 5.5 and in the next chapter. The technology is developing at a tremendously rapid pace and these exercises have been able to outline only a few of the methods employed.

4 Figure 5.4.2 is a diagram showing the steps involved in making recombinant bacteria, as described in this and the previous exercise. Select from the items A to M below the most suitable labels for boxes 1 to 12 in the diagram.

A   Small linear fragments.
B   Make gene *de novo*.
C   Cut plasmid with restriction enzyme.
D   Make double stranded cDNA from RNA.
E   Recircularised or uncut plasmids.
F   Mix plasmids with DNA fragments.
G   Grow cells on tetracycline medium.
H   Large molecules of many fragments joined together.
J   Cut total DNA with restriction enzyme.
K   Grow cells on ampicillin medium.
L   Make sticky ends.
M   Recombinant plasmids.

5 (a) How would the scheme shown in figure 5.4.2 have to be modified if the restriction enzyme used were *Pst* I? (See figure 5.3.1.)
    (b) Briefly explain how you would find the bacteria containing the recombinant plasmids.

5.5 *Recombinant DNA in perspective*

In recombinant DNA work the general aim is to genetically alter an organism by inserting foreign DNA in such a way that it will multiply as the cells multiply. The greatest advances have been made with bacteria. Here, the aim might be to improve a function which the microorganism already performs, for instance, converting cheap organic materials into protein for animal feed. Alternatively, recombinant DNA technology might be employed in the production of particular proteins, hitherto available only in small amounts. However, the purpose of the majority of recombinant DNA work at the present time is to obtain desired pieces of DNA in quantities sufficient for use in further investigations. The applications of the new technology are many and varied; the next section describes only a few of them.

Applications

Creating the right conditions for foreign genes to work inside bacteria is much more difficult than was at first imagined but recombinant bacteria are now being used in the manufacture of marketable amounts of useful proteins, such as human insulin. Currently, diabetics are treated with insulin derived from cows and pigs killed for meat. Pig insulin differs from human by only one amino acid but this difference is sufficient for the body's defence mechanisms to recognise it as a foreign substance and make antibodies against it. The consequences are that the patient needs larger doses to counterbalance neutralisation by antibodies, the site of injection becomes swollen and painful, and the insulin–antibody reaction may be responsible for some of the complications occasionally encountered. Despite unsuspected difficulties, insulin production by recombinant bacteria carrying the human gene was achieved by 1980 and it is now in commercial production. However, the impact of this achievement is diminished by the development of a simple and cheap method of modifying the amino acid sequence of pig insulin to make it indistinguishable from the human protein.

A number of human products are valuable or potentially so in the treatment of disease but are available from human tissues in very small quantities. Haemophiliacs lack the blood clotting substance, factor VIII, and are treated with a preparation derived from human blood. This source exposes patients to the risk of viral infections such as hepatitis B and AIDS while factor VIII produced by recombinant bacteria should be free of such contamination.

Interferons are proteins that are part of the body's defence against virus diseases and were thought to have potential in the treatment of cancer. Interferons are produced by white blood cells but until the genes were cloned in 1980 it had been impossible to get enough pure interferon to conduct adequate clinical trials. Now, much is known about different kinds of interferons and the genes which produce them as well as their value in treating disease. They have not turned out to be a wonder drug but they are effective in treating certain kinds of cancer and virus diseases.

One of the most successful areas of application of recombinant DNA technology is in the production of vaccines, especially those against viruses. An animal responds to infection by making antibodies against foreign molecules (antigens). With conventional vaccination, a dead or weakened form of the pathogen is injected into the animal where it cannot cause disease but its antigens are just as effective in stimulating antibody formation. Vaccination is not without risk, to the person or animal who receives it, should the vaccine be accidentally virulent, and to the personnel involved in vaccine manufacture. In addition, viral vaccines are expensive to produce because the viruses must be grown in live animal cells.

Recombinant DNA technology allows the production of cheaper and safer vaccines. All that is necessary to stimulate the immune response is the introduction of antigen into the body. Purified antigen can be extracted, using monoclonal antibodies, from bacteria into which virus antigen genes have been engineered. The virulent virus does not have to be grown at all during the production stage and the bacteria are easily and cheaply cultured. The vaccine consists of antigen only so there is little risk of contamination with virulent pathogen. Recombinant DNA methods are now employed on a commercial scale in the manufacture of vaccines against foot and mouth disease of cattle, scours (a diarrhoeic disease of cattle and pigs) and hepatitis B, a liver disease of humans. Any vaccine against AIDS will probably be produced using recombinant DNA technology.

1 In the passage above, find references to three different kinds of antigen/antibody reactions.

2 Use the information to complete a table with the following headings.

Useful products from genetically engineered bacteria

Product	Use	Conventional source	Advantages of recombinant DNA methods of production

Molecular genetics itself has been the primary beneficiary of the new technology. Before the era of gene cloning, genes could be studied only indirectly, by observing their phenotypic effects and at best by examining their immediate product. Now it is possible to isolate genes and work out the sequence of bases which makes up the whole functional unit.

It would be an enormous but not impossible task to determine the base sequence of any organism's entire genome but of more immediate interest is information on particular genes, such as, in humans, those associated with inherited diseases and cancer. Exercise 5.4 explained how gene probes are used to locate a gene; once an appropriate probe is available, any gene can be found in the genome of any organism. Gene probing and other applications of recombinant DNA technology to the study of human genetics will be described in chapter 6.

Limitations

The first artificial recombinant DNA molecule was cloned in 1974 and only a decade later, a multitude of small biotechnology firms were engaged in developing recombinant DNA methods to make useful products. The applications described above are a sample of those at the most advanced stage of development. Many other products are on the way but are still being tested before release on to the market. Progress has been rapid, despite hindrance by many unforseen difficulties, some of which have been described in exercise 5.2.

Even where bacteria can be engineered to produce satisfactory amounts of a desired gene product there remain problems to be overcome. One of the major difficulties is natural selection. What is to us a useful product means extra energy expenditure and reduced growth rate in the bacterium making it. In commercial production bacteria are grown in large vats called fermenters where there may be 10^{14} bacteria in 1000 litres of culture medium. With such huge numbers, it is not unlikely that at least one bacterium will lose its foreign genes. Relieved of its burden, this variant then multiplies faster than its encumbered cohabitants, eventually replacing them.

Another problem concerns recovery of the required product. Extraction of a pure protein is difficult and even trace amounts of a toxic contaminant can make a product unsuitable for use. Extraction is made easier if the bacteria secrete the desired protein into the surrounding medium and special techniques are available to make *E. coli* do this.

Many eukaryote proteins function poorly without the addition of sugar groups (glycosylation), a process which normally occurs in the endoplasmic reticulum and golgi apparatus. Bacteria do not glycosylate proteins, but yeast (a eukaryote) is able to carry out post-translational modifications such as this. Yeast is easy to culture on a large scale and work is in progress to develop it as an agent for gene cloning. In fact, genetically engineered yeast and mammal cell cultures will probably replace bacteria as agents for pharmaceutical protein production.

Further limitations are of an economic nature. The research necessary to produce satisfactory recombinant organisms is not particularly costly; the greatest expense is in scaling up processes for commercial production. Some products, like human growth hormone, are needed in such small quantities that drug companies may consider production to be uneconomical. If drugs are unprofitable, vaccines are even more likely to be so. Initially the demand for an effective vaccine will be high but as the pathogen finds fewer hosts in which to reproduce, the disease will become less frequent and the demand for the vaccine will fall. Another factor in the reckoning is that countries which could most benefit from new vaccines, say against malaria, are least able to pay.

Reports are beginning to appear in the scientific literature of the successful gene manipulation of plants such as tobacco and maize using recombinant DNA techniques. So far these have been genes which are easy to identify in the transformed plants rather than genes contributing to important economic traits. The majority of characters of economic importance in both plants and animals are controlled by many genes, whose number, locations and gene products are at present totally unknown. Most likely to succeed are those attempts to transfer single genes but even here there are difficulties in getting DNA into the cells in such a way that it is expressed in the right tissues and without interfering with other genes. When these difficulties have been overcome there remains the problem of growing whole animals or plants from genetically manipulated cells. Revolutionary as it is, recombinant DNA technology can only supplement conventional methods of genetic manipulation; it will not replace them.

3 Suggestions have been made that genetic engineering might be used to

- (i) transfer a gene for a powerful toxin into *E. coli*;
- (ii) transfer a gene for herbicide resistance into a crop plant;
- (iii) transfer the seventeen genes for nitrogen fixation from nitrogen fixing bacteria into cereals such as rice, wheat and maize;
- (iv) create a race of submissive people;
- (v) create calves with six legs;
- (vi) create calves with double the normal growth rate.

(a) For each item (i) to (vi) suggest a reason for wishing to achieve that aim.

(b) Say whether you think it is possible or improbable that each one will be achieved and give a reason.

Regulations

E. coli was and still is the favoured host for recombinant DNA and *E. coli* lives in the human gut as a natural symbiont. In a shotgun experiment, there is little control over what DNA is being cloned. What if a clone of highly pathogenic *E. coli* were made by accident, then escaped and caused an epidemic for which no drugs were available? Once released into the environment it might be impossible to eradicate the bacteria because they are self-replicating. What is more, they might pass on their recombinant plasmids by conjugation with other species of bacteria.

In the early days of recombinant DNA work, scientists knew they had the power to create organisms which had never before existed. They were so concerned that they might accidentally create something dangerous that in 1975 they called a meeting to discuss the regulation of their own experiments. As a result of this meeting the **Recombinant Advisory Group** (RAG) in the United States and the **Genetic Manipulation Advisory Group** (GMAG) in Britain were instituted to draw up guidelines for future experiments. The scientists agreed to two kinds of control, called **physical containment** and **biological containment**. Experiments were to be carried out under the same kind of secure physical conditions in which already known pathogens are handled and they would use as hosts for the recombinant DNA, 'disabled' *E. coli*, i.e. a strain which can only live in special culture conditions provided by a laboratory. The plasmids used as vectors would be made incapable of bringing about conjugation, by removal of the appropriate genes.

As research has progressed and the limitations of the work have become more apparent, there has been some relaxation of the controls on laboratory experiments but scientists must still seek approval for recombinant DNA work from safety committees. Concern remains, however, regarding the release of genetically engineered organisms into the environment. What would happen, for instance, if bacteria engineered to digest oil were released to clear up an oil spill and then took up residence in oil wells or internal combustion engines? Approval has been recently given for the restricted release of a genetically engineered virus which is toxic to certain species of caterpillars and also of a bacterium capable of reducing frost damage in crops. The potential impact of the new organisms on the ecosystem is being carefully assessed. The caution being exercised is understandable in the light of ecological catastrophes like the introduction of the rabbit into Australia; but haven't people been releasing genetically manipulated organisms into the environment ever since the beginning of agriculture? It is just that we now have new ways of making them.

4 Argue for or against the following objections to genetic engineering.
   (i) Transferring genes from one species into another is unnatural.
   (ii) It is not right that we should know so much about the laws of nature.
   (iii) We should not interfere with evolution by creating new life forms.
   (iv) Genetic engineers may accidentally create a monster no one can control.

6 Human variation

Introduction

The total human gene pool consists of all the alleles at every gene locus in the human species and each one of us carries just a tiny fraction. In the gene pool, some alleles are very common and others are rare. Common alleles occur in a large proportion of people and may owe their high frequency to the fact that they are either advantageous in certain environments or at least not disadvantageous. They contribute to the normal range of genetically determined individual differences in both quantitative and qualitative characters. Genes which are responsible for harmful inherited conditions occur at low frequencies because people born with these conditions tend to die young and are therefore unlikely to pass on their genes. Not all rare genes are harmful in their phenotypic effects and genes that are rare in some parts of the world are common in others. The human species is probably the most widespread of all and it is not surprising to find that allele frequencies are not distributed evenly over the inhabited earth (exercise 6.1).

Normal variation (exercises 6.2 to 6.4)

No two people are exactly alike; even genetically identical (monozygotic) twins differ in some respects as a result of environmental factors. In chapter 1 we saw how, in populations of animals and plants, it is possible to partition phenotypic variation into genetic and environmental components. One cannot, of course, carry out similar controlled crosses in humans but there are means of estimating heritabilities of human quantitative characters. Additive genetic variance is difficult to

measure in human populations and so normally estimates are made of the degree of genetic determination (also called 'heritability in the broad sense'). The values shown in table 6.1 are derived from studies on different populations and using various methods of estimation.

Table 6.1 *Approximate heritabilities of some human characters*

Character	Heritability
Height	0.8–0.9
Weight	0.4–0.8
Foot length	0.8
Total ridge count (fingerprints)	0.96
Blood pressure	0.7–0.8

Few people would argue over the validity of the heritability values given in table 6.1 but the same cannot be said for certain behavioural characteristics; much debate, the so-called 'nature–nurture' controversy, has centred around heritability estimates for intelligence.

Intelligence is measured by one's performance in practical or pencil-and-paper tests, the score being called the intelligence quotient (IQ). An intelligence test is supposed to measure an ability which is independent of socio-economic status or cultural background but few, if any, tests have escaped the criticism of cultural bias. The first source of uncertainty therefore is the definition and measurement of the character called intelligence.

A second difficulty is determining how much of the variation in IQ is due to genetic differences ('nature') and how much is due to environmental influences ('nurture'). The two sources of variation are difficult to separate because people who are related genetically often also share a similar environment. Recent investigations, carefully designed to avoid the bias of earlier studies, suggest a heritability for IQ of about 0.5.

A third factor in the controversy is interpretation of the term heritability. A value of 0.5 means that 50% of the variation in the population is due to genetic differences. It says nothing about the relative contribution of genes and environment to the expression of the character in an individual. It is ridiculous, for instance, to say that 50% of your intelligence is inherited and the other 50% is due to your environment. It is an equally mistaken belief that because a character has a high heritability, it is insensitive to environmental modification. The problem of 'nature *versus* nurture' is less controversial now that psychologists have a clearer understanding of the interaction between genetic and environmental factors affecting behaviour.

If we were asked to describe what makes a person unique, we would reply in terms of readily observable behaviour or physical features, whether environmental or genetic in origin. Using special techniques, individual differences may also be detected at the level of the gene product or even in the DNA itself. Variation in blood groups, for example, has been known since the beginning of this century when Landsteiner discovered the ABO system. A further dozen or more blood group systems have since been discovered. Blood groups are determined by proteins on the red blood cells and the presence or absence of the various proteins is detected by an antigen/antibody reaction. On addition of a certain antibody to a blood sample, the red blood cells will agglutinate (stick together) if they possess the corresponding antigenic protein in their membranes.

In the 1950s it was found that white blood cells too have antigens on their surface. These are not the same proteins as the red cell antigens but are also polymorphic. The group of closely linked genes which determines them is called the **HLA system** (HLA stands for human leucocyte or lymphocyte antigen). The proteins specified by the HLA system occur on nearly all body cells as well as leucocytes but not on red blood cells. Differences in these antigens are responsible for the rejection of tissue grafts; for this reason they are known as **histocompatibility antigens**.

Individual differences in proteins are a reflection of genetic differences but it is now possible, using recombinant DNA technology, to look at variation in the DNA itself. In 1980 a region of the human genome was found which consisted of a certain sequence of bases repeated many times. The significance of this finding lies in the fact that the number of repeats varies in different people. In the next five years Alec Jeffreys at Leicester University found many such variable regions scattered throughout the human genome. Using the appropriate restriction enzymes, these segments of DNA can be cut out, separated according to size by electrophoresis and made visible using radioactive probes. The resulting pattern (figure 6.1) is different for every individual and has become known as a **DNA fingerprint**. Towards the end of the last century, the investigation of crime greatly benefited from Francis Galton's discovery of the individuality of dermal ridges (fingerprints). Alec Jeffreys' technique of DNA fingerprinting marks the beginning of another revolution in forensic science. A DNA fingerprint can be made from a very small sample of blood or semen which can be as old as four years or more. In 1986 evidence from DNA fingerprinting was first accepted in a court of law; this was the first time that genetic evidence had been used to positively identify a person. This powerful new tool in the investigation of crime is, incidentally, a product of 'pure' research into molecular genetics.

Abnormal variation (exercises 6.5 to 6.7)

Here, abnormal variation refers to genetically

Figure 6.1 *DNA fingerprints; the 10 columns are the genetic fingerprints of 10 people, two of whom are identical twins (T); the scale shows the size (in kilobases) of the DNA fragments*

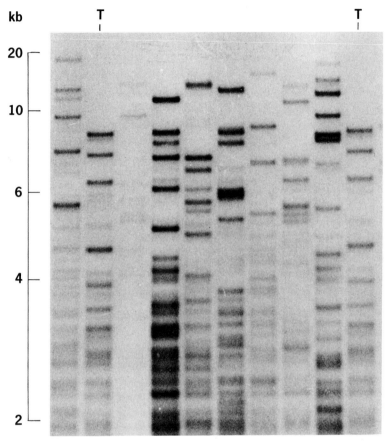

determined disorders which can affect the health and may reduce the reproductive fitness of the affected individual unless special treatment is given. At one extreme are those conditions, especially gross changes in chromosome constitution, which cause death at a very early stage of development and for which no treatment is possible. At the other extreme are conditions which manifest themselves only in certain environments, and treatment or prevention of symptoms is simply to avoid exposing oneself to the environments which elicit them.

About 1 in 2000 Europeans do not possess an enzyme which breaks down a commonly used muscle relaxant in general anaesthesia. Such a person is discovered to be 'abnormal' only when he or she is unusually slow to recover from a general anaesthetic. Another example of 'abnormal' genetic variation was brought to light with the introduction of primaquine as an antimalarial drug. People with a deficiency of the enzyme glucose-6-phosphate dehydrogenase (G-6-PD) in their red blood cells develop anaemia after treatment with this drug. G-6-PD deficiency is now known to be responsible for an acute anaemia called favism which develops in some people after eating broad beans *Vicia faba.*

Genetic diseases which, not so long ago, were fatal or severe enough to prevent reproduction can now be treated. **Phenylketonuria (PKU)** and **galactosaemia** are examples of hereditary diseases known as **inborn errors of metabolism**. In both diseases, lack of an enzyme results in toxic levels of a metabolite in the blood, phenylalanine (an amino acid abundant in some dairy products) in PKU and galactose phosphate (from lactose in milk) in galactosaemia. The symptoms of the diseases, which include severe mental retardation, can be avoided completely if the child is raised from birth on a diet low in the compound that he or she cannot metabolise. The diet can be relaxed after about ten years when brain growth is complete. Both diseases are caused by (different) recessive autosomal genes. PKU is one of the more common inborn errors of metabolism with an incidence in Europe and the USA of about 1 in 10 000 births and a heterozygote frequency of 1 in 50. (Heterozygotes for diseases determined by recessive genes are called **carriers**.) Because PKU can be successfully treated if diagnosed early, the blood of newborn babies is routinely checked for high levels of phenylalanine. Checking newborn babies for a hereditary disease is known as **population screening**. Successful treatment of the disease means that selection against the PKU gene has been relaxed because the 0.0001% of people who are homozygotes are as likely to reproduce as anyone else. However, considering that 99% of PKU genes are present in healthy heterozygotes, any rise in the allele frequency as a result of relaxed selection will be very slow indeed.

Genetic counselling

A number of hereditary blood disorders are common amongst certain ethnic groups because of a history of natural selection in favour of the genes responsible (see exercise 6.6). Sickle cell anaemia and thalassaemia are serious, often fatal, forms of anaemia which are a consequence of abnormal or insufficient haemoglobin. Sufferers are homozygotes and produce no normal haemoglobin. Heterozygotes on the other hand, enjoy normal health and often do not know that they are carriers.

Common experience tells us that some diseases 'run in the family' but it takes specialist knowledge to assess the risk that any unaffected person in the family will have an affected child. This is the job of a **genetic counsellor** who is usually a professional medical geneticist or a doctor specialising in children's diseases (a paediatrician). In general, people who seek genetic counselling are either themselves affected or have a close relative who is affected with a disease which *may* be hereditary. One of the first tasks of the counsellor is to determine whether the condition is hereditary at all. Drugs like thalidomide taken in pregnancy can cause deformity of the foetus but the deformity cannot be passed on to future generations because it is totally environmentally determined. Many hereditary abnormal conditions such as cleft lip (sometimes called hare lip) are under polygenic control and are also subject to environmental variation. If a condition is due to a single dominant or recessive autosomal or sex linked gene, the risks can be calculated using simple Mendelian genetics, but even then, the task is not as straightforward as exercise 6.7 might suggest.

Many people asking for genetic counselling are themselves healthy but run a high risk of being carriers of a hereditary disease. For many conditions caused by a recessive gene, there is no way of recognising heterozygotes. A couple only know for certain that they are both carriers when they produce an affected child and then they can be advised of the risk that their next child will be affected. If they decide to have another child, prenatal tests for some disorders are available. Some parents may ask for a termination of pregnancy if the foetus is found to be affected. The test normally involves removal of some of the amniotic fluid surrounding the foetus by

(a) Amniocentesis

Figure 6.2 *Procedures for prenatal diagnosis of genetic disease*

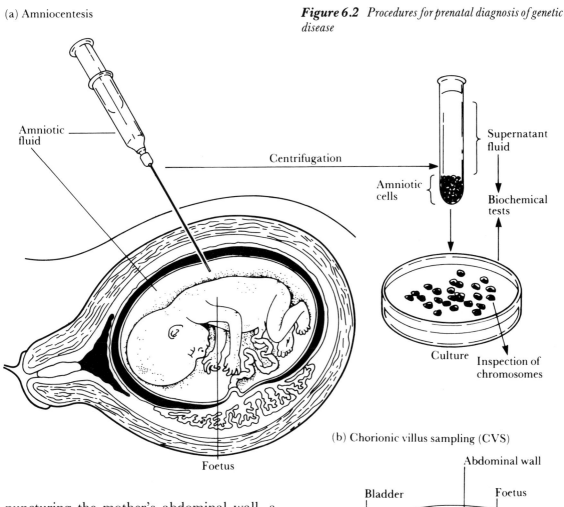

(b) Chorionic villus sampling (CVS)

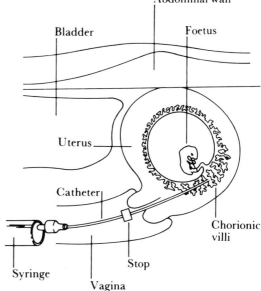

puncturing the mother's abdominal wall, a procedure called **amniocentesis** (figure 6.2 (a)). Biochemical tests are then performed either on the fluid itself or on cell cultures derived from foetal skin cells suspended in it. Cell culture following amniocentesis is necessary for prenatal diagnosis of chromosome abnormalities.

Unfortunately, amniocentesis cannot be performed satisfactorily until after fifteen weeks' gestation and if cell culture is necessary, a final result may be as late as eighteen weeks into the pregnancy. There is now a new procedure, called **chorionic villus sampling (CVS)** which allows prenatal diagnosis as early as eight weeks. Cell samples are obtained from the chorionic villi, i.e. the embryo's side of the developing placenta; both embryo and chorion are derived from the zygote so they are genetically identical. Figure 6.2 (b) shows how the cells are extracted by passing a tube through the cervix and into the womb; ultrasound scanning is used to help to guide the tip of the tube to the chorionic villi. Because they are actively dividing, chorionic villus cells can be observed directly for chromosome abnormalities; they do not necessarily have to be cultured and so the result of the test may be available within 24 hours.

A carrier of an autosomal recessive condition is at risk of having an affected child only if his or her spouse is also a carrier (or affected). Women who are heterozygous for a sex linked disorder such as Duchenne muscular dystrophy or haemophilia are at risk of having affected sons regardless of whom they marry. Although some carriers of Duchenne muscular dystrophy have higher levels of creatine kinase in the blood, there is so much variation in 'normal' levels that carrier status cannot be definitely determined from such tests.

Recombinant DNA technology promises to revolutionise both carrier detection and prenatal diagnosis. For an ever increasing number of single gene disorders, presence of the defective gene can be determined by investigation of the DNA itself. For prenatal diagnosis, DNA can be obtained either by amniocentesis or by CVS. For postnatal diagnosis or carrier detection sufficient DNA is obtained from a small (20 cm³) blood sample.

After the DNA has been extracted from the cells, it is cut up using restriction enzymes. The fragments are then separated by electrophoresis and transferred from the fragile gel to a piece of tough nitrocellulose filter paper. Amongst all the DNA on the filter paper is the gene of interest and we find it by using a **radioactive gene probe**, as described in exercise 5.4. Obtaining a suitable probe is the most difficult part of this technique. If the

amino acid sequence of the gene product is known, e.g. haemoglobin and some enzymes, then a cDNA probe can be made; otherwise one can be made from DNA in a gene library (see exercise 5.3) derived from an affected person. Gene probes are already available for Duchenne muscular dystrophy, G-6-PD deficiency, Huntington's disease, PKU, sickle cell anaemia, thalassaemia, cystic fibrosis and several other genetic disorders.

Medical applications of recombinant DNA technology go beyond the drugs and vaccines produced by recombinant bacteria. For many genetic disorders, the new technology allows heterozygotes to be identified with a high degree of probability and so advice can be given with greater accuracy on the risk of having an affected child. As for prenatal diagnosis, DNA obtained by CVS allows precise determination of an embryo's genotype early in development so that a termination, if requested, can be carried out after only a few weeks of pregnancy. Identification and cloning of individual genes means that their base sequences can be analysed and it is already possible to see exactly the nature of the mutation in some deleterious alleles. This could give us insight into ways of treating diseases such as cystic fibrosis where the defective gene product is unknown.

At present, strategies for combating genetic disease include advising parents of the risk of having an affected baby and making termination available, and, secondly, treating the symptoms of sufferers. Only a few hereditary diseases, like PKU and galactosaemia, are in any sense curable. It is most unlikely that genetic disease will be cured by repairing defective DNA. Even though it is theoretically possible to manipulate the DNA of an abnormal embryo, it is far more straightforward to abort the embryo and hope for a normal pregnancy next time. Although some people object to abortion on principle, they would probably object even more to the *in vitro* genetic manipulation of a human embryo.

Gene therapy might be possible with some

of the blood disorders, especially sickle cell anaemia and thalassaemia where the abnormality is in the synthesis of haemoglobin in the bone marrow. One idea, which has been attempted in the treatment of thalassaemia, is to remove some of the patient's bone marrow, to introduce into these cells cloned genes for normal globin and then to put the genetically engineered bone marrow back into the patient. The first trials, in 1980, unfortunately failed, probably because the globin genes were not incorporated into a suitable position in the host DNA. If the technique could be made to work, the individual sufferer could be cured but would remain capable of transmitting the defective gene to the next generation as it would still be present in all his or her gametes. In the future, some single gene disorders may be curable by removing, engineering and replacing liver cells but, as yet, not enough is known about the molecular basis of the majority of genetically determined diseases to make gene therapy possible. Disorders with a heritable component account for about half of all deaths in childhood. Any major reduction in the incidence of genetic disease will come from the application of recombinant DNA technology to prenatal diagnosis and carrier detection rather than to the treatment of sufferers already born.

6.1 Geographical variation in blood groups

Since the ABO blood groups were discovered early this century a great deal of information has been collected on their world wide distribution. In the ABO system there are four blood groups, controlled by three different alleles at the same gene locus. The alleles are I^O, I^A and I^B. Blood group O is genotype $I^O I^O$ and group AB is genotype $I^A I^B$. Group A is genotype $I^A I^O$ or $I^A I^A$ and group B is $I^B I^O$ or $I^B I^B$. The alleles vary in frequency over different parts of the world with allele I^O being the most common; nowhere in the world is it less than

50%. I^A is the next most common allele and reaches its highest frequency, of 55%, in the Lapps of North Norway and Finland. Central Asia and the Far East have the highest frequency of I^B, at 30%.

If the allele frequencies in a population are known, the Hardy–Weinberg equation allows genotype frequencies to be calculated. You should be familiar with the Hardy–Weinberg equation for two alleles, say A and a. The equation is
$$p^2 + 2pq + q^2 = 1$$
where p^2 is the frequency of the genotype AA,
 $2pq$ is the frequency of the genotype Aa,
and q^2 is the frequency of the genotype aa.

1 In this question, let q be the frequency of I^O and let p equal the frequency of the other alleles taken together. In a sample of over 12 000 Japanese, the frequency of I^O was 0.56. What percentage of this population are blood group O?

In any population where all three alleles exist, people who are not blood group O are group A, group B or group AB. It is possible to calculate the frequency of all four genotypes from a knowledge of allele frequencies using a modification of the Hardy–Weinberg equation. In table 6.1.1, the square represents a population. The sides of the square are divided in proportion to the frequency of alleles I^O, I^A and I^B. The smaller squares and rectangles in the larger square represent the proportion of the population with the different genotypes.

Table 6.1.1 *Diagram showing the proportions of different blood group genotypes in a population*

Spermatozoa

		$p(I^O)$	$q(I^A)$	$r(I^B)$
Ova	$p(I^O)$	$p^2(I^O I^O)$		
	$q(I^A)$	$pq(I^O I^A)$		
	$r(I^B)$	$pr(I^O I^B)$		

2 In table 6.1.1, some of the genotypes and their proportions have been filled in for you. Copy out the square and complete the blank sections.

The completed table shows that when there are three alleles at a locus the Hardy–Weinberg equation is

$$p^2 + 2pq + 2\,pr + q^2 + 2qr + r^2 = 1$$

The terms in the equation give genotype frequencies and the corresponding genotypes should be shown in your table. Use this table to help you answer question 3.

3 Find the percentage of the genotypes I^OI^O, I^OI^A, I^OI^B, I^AI^A, I^AI^B and I^BI^B in the following populations.

	p = freq. I^O	q = freq. I^A	r = freq. I^B
(a) New Zealand (Maoris)	0.66	0.32	0.02
(b) Thailand (Bangkok)	0.61	0.16	0.23
(c) Ecuador (Indians)	0.97	0.02	0.01

4 What is the percentage of the blood groups A, B, O and AB in each of the populations in question 3?

6.2 *Continuous variation*

Sheffield school pupils aged 17–18 years were asked to measure the length of their middle fingers from knuckle to fingertip on their own hands and on their mother's and father's hands. Data were collected from 30 girls and 20 boys and their parents. Middle fingers are not necessarily the same length on both hands so the average finger length was calculated for each person. The variation in the mothers and in the fathers is shown in figure 6.2.1.

1 Is the variation in finger length within the group of mothers and within the group of fathers due to genetic differences, environmental differences or both?

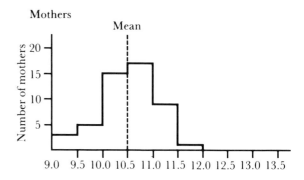

Figure 6.2.1 *Variation in finger length in 50 mothers and fathers of 17- to 18-year-old school pupils*

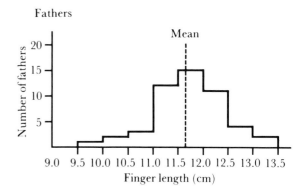

2 How can you account for the difference between mothers and fathers in mean finger length?

Figure 6.2.2 shows the extent of the resemblance between daughters and their parents. Each girl's finger length has been plotted against the mean finger length of her parents. The dots are scattered but there is a general tendency for parents with long fingers to have long fingered daughters and parents with short fingers to have short fingered daughters. The gradient of the line which best fits all the points is shown on the graph and is a measure of the degree of resemblance between parents and offspring, that is, the heritability. The heritability of finger length according to this graph is 0.89.

Figure 6.2.2 *Graph showing the similarity of finger length in parents and daughters*

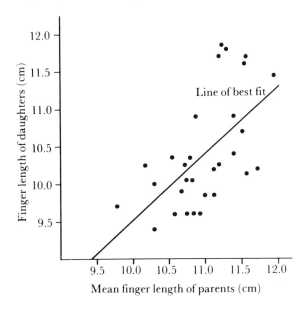

3 Which one of the following is a valid conclusion from this experiment?
   A   89% of fingers in Sheffield are genetically determined.
   B   Finger length in some Sheffield school pupils is 89% determined by genes.
   C   89% of human genes determine finger length.
   D   89% of variation in finger length in a small British population is genetically determined.
   E   11% of variation in finger length is due to environmental differences between people.

6.3 A question of paternity

Genetical evidence is sometimes used in a court of law, in particular, in attempts to settle a dispute as to who is or is not the father of a particular child. The evidence is normally based on the blood groups of mother, child and putative father. Blood group evidence can only eliminate a man as the father; it cannot prove that he is the father. The more blood groups tested, the more likely it is that a man who is not the father can be eliminated. Three of the most commonly used blood groups are shown in table 6.3.1. The blood group is the phenotype and this may or may not allow the genotype to be precisely determined. Phenotypes and corresponding genotypes are given in the table below.

Table 6.3.1 *Phenotypes and corresponding genotypes for three blood group systems*

System	Alleles	Phenotypes	Genotypes
ABO	I^A, I^B, I^O	A	$I^A I^A$, $I^A I^O$
		B	$I^B I^B$, $I^B I^O$
		O	$I^O I^O$
		AB	$I^A I^B$
Rhesus	D, d	Rhesus +	DD, Dd
		Rhesus −	dd
MN	L^M, L^N	M	$L^M L^M$
		N	$L^N L^N$
		MN	$L^M L^N$

1 Due to an oversight, two baby girls born in a hospital on the same night were not properly identified before being taken to the nursery. The next day, no one was certain which baby belonged to which parents so blood tests were done on the two couples and the two babies. The results were as in table 6.3.2.

Table 6.3.2

	ABO group	Rhesus group	MN group
Mr S	O	+	MN
Mrs S	O	+	M
Mr T	O	+	MN
Mrs T	A	+	MN
Baby X	O	+	N
Baby Z	O	−	MN

(a) Which baby belongs to Mr and Mrs T?
(b) What is the blood group evidence which enabled your decision?

2 What blood groups must a man possess which would exclude him from being the father in each of the cases (a) and (b) below?

Mother's phenotype Child's phenotype
(a) A, Rhesus +, MN   O, Rhesus +, N
(b) O, Rhesus −, N   A, Rhesus +, N

Table 6.3.3 *The frequencies of the ABO, Rhesus and MN blood groups in Britain*

System	Phenotype	Frequency (%)
ABO	O	46
	A	42
	B	9
	AB	3
Rhesus	+	84
	−	16
MN	MN	50
	M	30
	N	20

3 Use the data given in table 6.3.3 to answer this question. In the following cases, what is the chance that a man who is not the father of the child will be excluded after a blood test?
(a) Mother and child are both group O.
(b) Mother is group N and baby is MN.
(c) Mother and child are both Rhesus negative.
(d) Mother is group B and baby is group A.

4 Possession of which blood group phenotype(s) can never exclude a man in a disputed paternity case whatever the blood groups of mother and child?

The new technique of DNA fingerprinting seems set to replace blood group evidence in questions of uncertain relationships. As explained in the introduction to this chapter, a DNA fingerprint is made by cutting up total human DNA with restriction endonucleases, subjecting the fragments to electrophoresis and using a radioactive probe to locate those fragments containing characteristic base sequences. These fragments are called 'minisatellites' and contain up to 500 or more repeats of a certain sequence of bases. The 'fingerprint' is a pattern of bands (see figure 6.1) containing DNA fragments separated by electrophoresis according to size; the smaller the fragment (i.e. the fewer the number of repeats), the further it moves through the gel. Each minisatellite is a piece from a single chromosome and so any band present in the DNA fingerprint of a child must also be present in at least one of the parents.

5 Figure 6.3.1 represents the DNA fingerprints of a girl (A), her parents, her sister and a number of other persons, two of whom are brothers and are unrelated to the first family. Identify the DNA fingerprints of
(a) the parents of girl A, (b) girl A's sister, (c) the two brothers.

Figure 6.3.1 *DNA fingerprints*

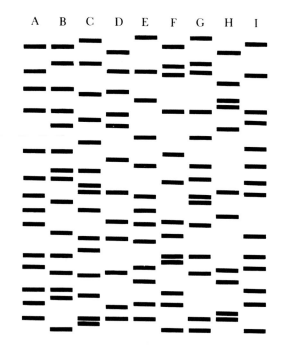

6.4 Self and non-self

One of the remarkable features of vertebrates is the ability of an individual to recognise cells which belong to it (self) and cells which do not (non-self). Foreign cells introduced into the body, whether pathogens or transplanted tissue, are attacked by antibodies produced by the host's lymphocytes. Foreign cells have molecules in their membranes, usually but not always proteins, which the host recognises as non-self. These molecules, which stimulate the production of antibodies, are called **antigens**. Exercise 6.3 is concerned with the blood group antigens, i.e. the antigens on red blood cells. This exercise is concerned with the HLA antigens that occur on most cells of the human body other than red blood cells. Incompatibility of the HLA antigens between donor and recipient is the major cause of rejection of skin and organ transplants. If a person needs a kidney transplant, for instance, a potential donor must have as near as possible the same HLA antigens as the recipient (as well as the same ABO blood group). This matching of donors and recipient is called **tissue typing**.

The HLA antigens are encoded by four closely linked genes on chromosome 6. The genes are called *HLA-A*, *HLA-B*, *HLA-C* and *HLA-D* and they code for 20 HLA-A, 40 HLA-B, 8 HLA-C and 12 HLA-D antigens respectively. The existence of so many different antigens of each type means that each gene has many alleles, each allele encoding one antigen. Any person can carry, at most, two different alleles at each gene locus. All the alleles are codominant so each person can have up to eight different HLA antigens on his or her cells.

1 For any one locus, the number of different genotypes possible is given by the formula $\frac{1}{2}n(n + 1)$, where n is the number of alleles. Calculate the number of different genotypes possible at the
(a) *HLA-A* locus (20 alleles),
(b) *HLA-B* locus (40 alleles),
(c) *HLA-C* locus (8 alleles),
(d) *HLA-D* locus (12 alleles).

2 Multiply together the four numbers calculated in question 1 to give the total number of different genotypes (and therefore combinations of antigens).

It will be clear from your answer to question 2 why it may be difficult to find a suitable donor for a transplant operation. The odds against are somewhat reduced by the fact that some alleles are more frequent than others. But even the most common allele in Europe (*A2* at the *HLA-A* locus) has a frequency of only 0.27. Perfect tissue matching between unrelated people is almost impossible but it has been found that some HLA antigens are much more powerful in evoking rejection. As long as these are the same in donor and recipient, a graft should be successful.

A donor for kidney or bone marrow is usually sought amongst the relatives of the patient. The four HLA loci are very closely linked so tend to be inherited as a block. Each block of genes is called a **haplotype** and they are rarely disturbed by crossing over (see figure 6.4.1).

3 In figure 6.4.1, how many different HLA antigens are present in (a) the father, (b) the mother?

Figure 6.4.1 *Inheritance of HLA haplotypes in a family*

Locus	Father		Mother		Son	
HLA-A	A3	A24	A2	A2	A24	A2
HLA-C	C6	C4	C1	C3	C4	C3
HLA-B	B27	B12	B13	B5	B12	B5
HLA-D	D3	D2	D6	D2	D2	D2

4 The parents in figure 6.4.1 also have a daughter. In your answers to the following questions, assume that there is no crossing over within the HLA region.
(a) What is the probability that the son and daughter

(i) have exactly the same HLA antigens;

(ii) have at least four of their HLA antigens in common;

(iii) have less than four HLA antigens in common?

(b) (i) How many antigens does the mother have which are not present in her son?

(ii) How many antigens does the father have which are not present in his son?

(c) The son needs a kidney transplant and his parents and sister are all willing to donate one of theirs should they prove to have a compatible tissue type. Assume that all the incompatible antigens are equally potent in bringing about rejection of the graft and the more similar the antigens in donor and recipient the longer the grafted tissue survives. Give reasons, based on HLA incompatibility alone, for choosing mother, father or sister as the donor.

6.5 *Chromosome abnormalities*

At least 7.5% of all conceptions have a chromosome abnormality and the great majority of these are spontaneously aborted (miscarried) or stillborn. About a quarter of chromosomally abnormal foetuses are triploid or tetraploid, another quarter have a chromosome missing and about half have an extra chromosome. The majority are eliminated by natural selection before the full period of gestation but about 6 in 1000 liveborn babies have a chromosomal abnormality.

About 1 in 700 livebirths has **Down's syndrome**, representing a survival rate of about 20%. This distinct type of mental subnormality and associated features was described by John Langdon-Down in 1866. In 1959 it was discovered that Down's syndrome patients have three copies of chromosome 21 in their cells instead of the normal two and the condition is now commonly called **trisomy 21** (figure 6.5.1). This, and the majority of other chromosome abnormalities are largely due to new mutations occurring either in the formation of the gametes or in the first mitotic divisions of the zygote. Most cases of trisomy 21 are a result of **non-disjunction** in the formation of the ovum. Non-disjunction means that either homologous chromosomes fail to separate during anaphase of the first meiotic division or chromatids fail to separate at anaphase of the second meiotic division, as illustrated in figure 6.5.2.

1 What is the chance that an ovum is abnormal if non-disjunction occurs
(a) in the first meiotic division,
(b) in the second meiotic division?

2 In trisomy 21 resulting from non-disjunction, all three chromosomes 21 are different or two are similar and one is different. Explain how these two conditions arise.

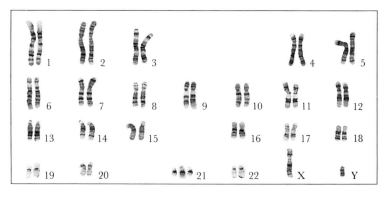

Figure 6.5.1 *Karotype of Down's syndrome (trisomy–21); a special staining technique called Giemsa banding allows identification of individual chromosomes*

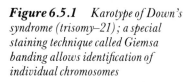

Since half the normal population does not suffer from having no Y-chromosome and the other half survives with only one X-chromosome, it is perhaps not surprising that sex chromosome abnormalities are fairly common. An extra sex chromosome in a male can give rise to the sex chromosome constitutions **XYY** and **XXY**, both of which occur with a frequency of about 1 in 1000 male births. XYY males tend to be taller than average but are otherwise normal. XXY (**Klinefelter's syndrome**) males have male external genitalia but the testes are small and fail to produce normal levels of testosterone. This leads to poorly developed secondary sexual characteristics and a tendency towards breast development. Intelligence may be low but is within the normal range. XXY men are infertile and

the majority are not diagnosed until adulthood when the reason for their infertility is investigated.

It is the presence or absence of a Y-chromosome which makes a person male or female, not the number of X-chromosomes. People with one X-chromosome and no other sex chromosome are female. This condition, called **Turner's syndrome**, occurs in about 1 in 2500 female livebirths but these represent only 1% of those conceived. Those who do survive to birth may not be recognisably abnormal but are diagnosed later as a result of investigation into the cause of their short stature and failure to develop secondary sexual characteristics. Turner's syndrome girls do not have ovaries and so are infertile. Their intelligence may be normal. The sex

Figure 6.5.2 *Non-disjunction of chromosome 21*

(a) Failure of homologues to separate at meiosis anaphase I

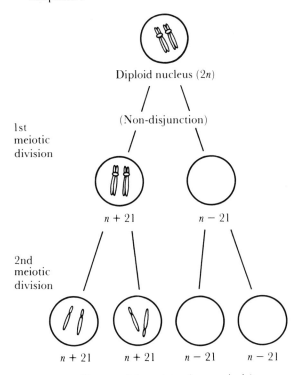

(b) Failure of chromatids to separate at meiosis anaphase II

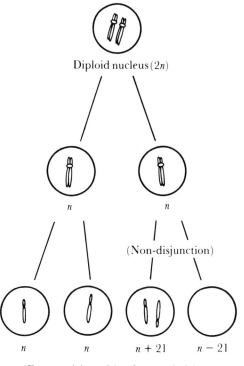

chromosome constitution in Turner's syndrome is represented **X0**. The corresponding condition, **Y0**, is unknown, presumably because the embryos are spontaneously aborted early in development.

Another sex chromosome abnormality, which occurs in 1 in 1000 female births, is **XXX**. A small proportion of such females have low intelligence and about a quarter are infertile but the majority are probably undiagnosed. All of the chromosome constitutions, XYY, XXY, X0, Y0 and XXX can occur as a result of non-disjunction during gamete formation.

3 Abnormal ova can result from non-disjunction of X-chromosomes at either the first or second meiotic divisions. What are the possible sex chromosome constitutions of zygotes produced as a result of fertilisation of abnormal ova by normal sperm if non-disjunction in the female occurs
 (a) in the first meiotic division,
 (b) in the second meiotic division?

4 Abnormal sperm can result from non-disjunction of sex chromosomes at either the first or second meiotic divisions. What are the possible sex chromosome constitutions of zygotes produced as a result of abnormal sperm fertilising normal ova if non-disjunction in the male occurs
 (a) in the first meiotic division,
 (b) in the second meiotic division?

6.6 *Genetics and malaria*

A serious and often fatal form of malaria, called malignant tertian malaria, is caused by the single celled parasite *Plasmodium falciparum*. It is transmitted from one person to another by female mosquitoes when they suck human blood.

Selection pressure imposed by a parasite on its host often brings about evolution of resistance (see chapter 4). Humanity and the malarial parasite have coexisted for thousands, perhaps millions, of years so it is not surprising to find genetically determined resistance to the disease. *Plasmodium* grows and reproduces inside red blood cells and depends for its nutrition on haemoglobin. It is adapted to feed on normal haemoglobin and grows less successfully or not at all in cells with certain abnormal forms of the protein. There are over 300 variants of human haemoglobin and some of these are known to confer resistance to malaria.

Haemoglobin contains four polypeptide chains, two identical α-chains and two identical β-chains. The α- and β-chains (or α- and β-globins) are produced by two separate gene loci. One of the abnormal haemoglobins, called haemoglobin S, has the amino acid valine instead of glutamic acid at the sixth position in the β-chain. This haemoglobin is coded for by the allele *Hb^s* and *Hb^sHb^s* homozygotes suffer from the disease called sickle cell anaemia. The frequency of *Hb^s* is high in some parts of Africa because heterozygotes are more resistant to malaria than are homozygotes for the normal allele.

Another type of anaemia, called thalassaemia, is genetically determined and common particularly in Mediterranean countries. The relatively high frequency of the genes responsible for this serious disease is probably because they confer resistance to malaria when heterozygous. A recent report estimates that worldwide 200 000 to 300 000 babies are born every year with sickle cell anaemia or a severe form of thalassaemia. Patients suffering from β-thalassaemia, who are homozygous for a recessive allele, produce little or no β-globin. They compensate for the lack of β-globin by the continued production of foetal haemoglobin but they usually die before reproducing even with medical treatment.

β-thalassaemia is the most widespread abnormality of haemoglobin production. Recombinant DNA technology has revealed a number of different alleles at the β-globin locus. In general, a person with any two abnormal alleles dies before reproducing. Heterozygotes carrying one normal allele are usually as healthy as people homozygous for the normal allele although some may have a mild form of anaemia.

1 (a) Imagine a population where the frequency of an allele for β-thalassaemia (*b*) is 0.1. Use the Hardy–Weinberg equation to calculate how many babies out of 1000 born would be
  (i) homozygous for the normal allele (*BB*),
  (ii) heterozygous (*Bb*),
  (iii) homozygous for thalassaemia (*bb*).

 (b) If all the babies are equally likely to grow to maturity and have children of their own, what would be the expected frequency of *b* in the next generation? (There is no need to calculate genotype frequencies in the next generation.)

 (c) If all the *bb* homozygotes die of thalassaemia before reproducing but *BB* and *Bb* individuals are equally likely to reproduce, what will be the expected frequency of *b* in the next generation?

 (d) All the *bb* homozygotes die of thalassaemia and 20% of *BB* homozygotes die of malaria before reproducing, but all the heterozygotes survive. If there is no difference in the reproductive rate of these and the surviving *BB* homozygotes, what will be the expected frequency of *b* in the next generation?

2 Explain how the frequency of *b* could remain fairly constant in parts of the world where malignant malaria is endemic.

3 Malaria has been eliminated from many parts of Europe where it was formerly common. What effect do you expect this to have on the frequency of alleles for β-thalassaemia?

6.7 *Single gene disorders*

Abnormalities of chromosome number so severely reduce the reproductive fitness of those individuals who carry them that the vast majority of such abnormalities are the result of new mutation occurring either in meiosis in the parent or in the mitotic divisions of the early embryo. New mutation is often responsible when an infant with a disease determined by an autosomal (i.e. not sex linked) dominant gene is born to normal parents. Such diseases include **neurofibromatosis** (multiple brown lumps in the skin) and **achondroplasia** (restricted growth). The mutation rate of neurofibromatosis is 1 in 10 000 gametes and that of achondroplasia is 14 per million gametes.

Amongst the most common hereditary diseases are those caused by X linked genes. The reason for their prevalence is that women can carry the gene in the heterozygous state with no effect on their reproductive ability but half their sons, on average, will be affected. Such diseases include **Duchenne muscular dystrophy** (figure 6.7.1) and **haemophilia**. Duchenne muscular dystrophy begins with muscle weakness in early childhood which becomes progressively more severe as the boy grows up, and as yet there is no treatment. Haemophilia, however, can be treated by replacing the missing blood clotting factor, and so it is possible for males as well as females to pass on the gene.

1 Queen Victoria's son Leopold suffered from haemophilia and at least two of her daughters were carriers. Victoria herself did not have the disease and neither did her husband Prince Albert, nor her parents, Edward, Duke of Kent, and Victoria of Saxe-Coburg. The gene inherited by Queen Victoria's children was probably a new mutation which arose during gamete formation. In which of the people listed on the next page could it have arisen during gamete formation?

A   Edward, Duke of Kent
B   Edward's mother (Queen Charlotte)
C   Victoria of Saxe-Coburg
D   Prince Albert
E   Queen Victoria
F   Prince Leopold

The most common autosomal recessive disorder in people of European descent is **cystic fibrosis**. One person in 23 is a carrier (i.e. heterozygous) and one child in 2000 is born with the condition. The disease is characterised by thick mucus which blocks the bronchioles and pancreatic duct, causing problems with breathing and digestion.

Huntington's disease is caused by an autosomal dominant gene but its symptoms, of uncontrolled movements, do not usually become apparent until after childbearing age. Consequently the disease is relatively common, having an incidence of 1 in 20 000.

2 Pedigrees of Huntington's disease, Duchenne muscular dystrophy and cystic fibrosis are shown in figure 6.7.2. Using the information given above, match each disease to one of the pedigrees and give reasons for your choices.

In the pedigrees each individual is identified by two numbers, the generation number (Roman numeral) and the number in that generation (Arabic numeral).

3 In pedigree A, what is the probability that the following persons are heterozygous: (a) the girl, III-5, (b) her aunt, II-4, (c) her uncle, II-3?

4 (a) In pedigree B, what is the probability that IV-1 is heterozygous?
   (b) II-9 died young. What is the probability that she was heterozygous?
   (c) III-4 is 40-years-old and showing no signs of the disease. If 30% of people who will develop symptoms have done so by the age of 40, calculate the probability that III-4 is heterozygous. (Find first the probability that he is heterozygous, then the probability that he is heterozygous but not showing symptoms.)

5 (a) In pedigree C, what is the probability that II-2 is heterozygous? (Use all the information in the pedigree.)
   (b) III-4 and III-5 plan to have another child but will consider having the pregnancy terminated if amniocentesis shows the foetus to be a boy.
      (i) What is the probability that the boy would be normal?

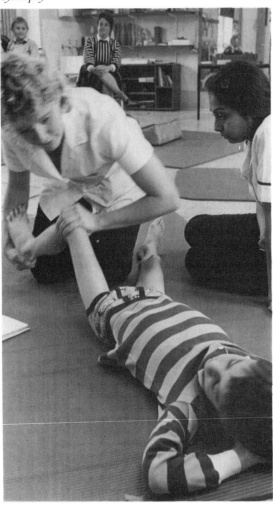

Figure 6.7.1 *Physiotherapy for a boy with muscular dystrophy*

(ii) How can amniocentesis reveal the sex of the foetus?

(c) IV-2 has just married and wants to start a family.

(i) What is the probability that she is a carrier of the disease?

(ii) If she has a son, what is the probability that he will be affected?

Figure 6.7.2 *Pedigrees showing the inheritance of three diseases (filled symbols represent affected individuals)*

Pedigree A

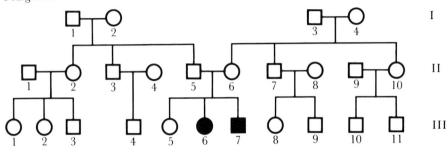

Pedigree B

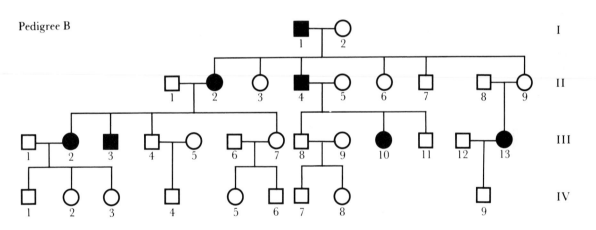

Pedigree C

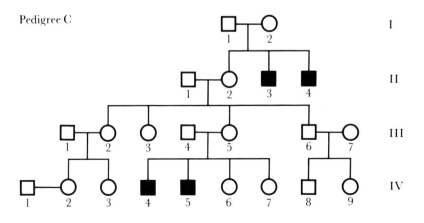

Suggestions for further reading

Chapters 1 and 2

Allard, R. W., *Principles of plant breeding*, John Wiley and Sons, 1960

Bowman, J. C., *An introduction to animal breeding*, 2nd ed., Edward Arnold, Studies in Biology no. 46, 1984

Brewbaker, J. L., *Agricultural genetics*, Prentice-Hall, 1964

Dalton, D. C., *An introduction to practical animal breeding*, 2nd ed., Collins, 1985

Ford-Lloyd, B. & M. Jackson, *Plant genetic resources: an introduction to their conservation and use*, Edward Arnold, 1986

Hammond Jr, J., J. C. Bowman & T. J. Robinson (revisers), *Hammond's farm animals*, 5th ed., Edward Arnold, 1983

Hutt, F. B. & B. A. Rasmusen, *Animal genetics*, 2nd ed., John Wiley & Sons, 1982

Land, J. B. & R. B. Land, *Food chains to biotechnology*, Thomas Nelson, 1983

Lasley, J. F., *Genetics of livestock improvement*, 4th ed., Prentice-Hall, Inc., 1987

Lawrence, W. J. C., *Plant breeding*, Edward Arnold, Studies in Biology no. 12, 1968

Lewis, D., *Sexual incompatibility in plants*, Edward Arnold, Studies in Biology no. 110, 1979

Simmonds, N. W., *Evolution of crop plants*, Longman, 1976

Simmonds, N. W., *Principles of crop improvement*, Longman, 1979

Watts, L., *Flower and vegetable plant breeding*, Grower Books, 1980

Welsh, J. R., *Fundamentals of plant genetics and breeding*, John Wiley and Sons, 1981

Chapters 3 and 4

Bishop, J. A. & L. M. Cook, *Genetic consequences of man-made change*, Academic Press, 1981

Conway, C. (ed.), *Pesticide resistance and world food production*, Imperial College Centre for Environmental Technology, 1982

Day, P. R., *Genetics of host–parasite interaction*, Freeman, 1974

Emden H. F. van, *Pest control and its ecology*, Edward Arnold, Studies in Biology no. 50, 1974

Pal, R. & M. J. Whitten, *The use of genetics in insect control*, Elsevier/North-Holland, 1974

Chapter 5

Ayala, F. J. & J. A. Kiger Jr, *Modern genetics*, 2nd ed., Benjamin Cummings, 1984

Brown, T. A., *Gene cloning, an introduction*, Van Nostrand Reinhold (UK), 1986

Cherfas, J., *Man made life*, Basil Blackwell, 1982

Drlica, K., *Understanding DNA and gene cloning. A guide for the curious*, John Wiley & Sons, 1984

Hardy, K., *Bacterial plasmids*, 2nd ed., Van Nostrand Reinhold (UK), 1986

Ingle, M. R., *Genetic mechanisms*, Basil Blackwell, 1986

Lin, E. C. C., R. Goldstein & M. Syvanen, *Bacteria, plasmids and phages*, Harvard University Press, 1984

Mantell, S. H., J. A. Matthews & R. A. McKee, *Principles of plant biotechnology*, Blackwell Scientific Publications, 1985

Nossal, G. J. V., *Reshaping life; key issues in genetic engineering*, Cambridge University Press, 1985

Strickberger, M. W., *Genetics*, 3rd ed., Collier Macmillan, 1985

Warr, J. R., *Genetic engineering in higher organisms*, Edward Arnold, Studies in Biology no. 162, 1984

Watson, J. D., J. Tooze & D. T. Kurtz, *Recombinant DNA, a short course*, Scientific American Books, 1983

Chapter 6

Bodmer, W. F. & L. L. Cavalli-Sforza, *Genetics, evolution and man*, W. H. Freeman & Co, 1976

Clarke, C. A., *Human genetics and medicine*, Edward Arnold, New Studies in Biology, 3rd ed., 1987

Connor, J. M. & M. A. Ferguson-Smith, *Essential medical genetics*, Blackwell, 1984

Edwards, J. H., *Human genetics*, Chapman and Hall, 1978

Emery, A. E. H., *An introduction to recombinant DNA*. John Wiley & Sons, 1984

Fraser-Roberts, J. A. & M. Pembrey, *An introduction to medical genetics*, Oxford University Press, 8th ed., 1985

Harper, P. S., *Practical genetic counselling*, Wright, Bristol, 2nd ed., 1984

Lerner, I. M. & W. J. Libby, *Heredity, evolution and society*, 2nd ed., W. H. Freeman & Co., 1976

Lewontin, R., *Human diversity*. Scientific American Books, 1982

Macleod, A. & K. Sikora, *Molecular biology and human disease*, Blackwell Scientific Publications, 1984

Milunsky, A., *Know your genes*, Pelican, 1980

Mourant, A. E., *Blood relations*, Oxford University Press, 1983

Weatherall, D., *The new genetics and clinical practice*, 2nd ed., Oxford University Press, 1985

Notes and answers to exercises

1 Introduction to quantitative genetics

1.1 Continuous variation (related exercises 2.4, 3.1 and 6.2)

1 (a) One

(b) Let r^1 represent the allele for red and let r^2 represent the allele for white. r^1r^1 is red, r^1r^2 is intermediate and r^2r^2 is white.

2 1:4:6:4:1

3 6 5 5 5 4 4 4 3
5 4 4 4 3 3 3 2
5 4 4 4 3 3 3 2
5 4 4 4 3 3 3 2
4 3 3 3 2 2 2 1
4 3 3 3 2 2 2 1
4 3 3 3 2 2 2 1
3 2 2 2 1 1 1 0

5 Six shades of red (plus white)

Sources of data: Treasury of human inheritance, Vol. II. Galton Laboratory, p. 428; L. F. Chao (1928) *Genetics* **13**: 133–69.

1.2 Environmental variation (related exercises 2.4, 4.2 and 6.2)

1 Almost certainly identical in monozygotic twins are (ii) and (iv). Fingerprints are usually very similar but not identical. All of the other characters are modifiable by the environment and therefore not necessarily identical in twins.

2 (a) Dwarf (b) Dwarf

3 3 short:1 long, with environmental variation

5 Genetic, because the two lines were grown under the same environmental conditions

6 The within-line variation is environmental in origin because all the seeds have the same genotype.

7 (a) 642 mg

(b) 642 mg. The lightest and heaviest seeds have the same genotype and are completely homozygous. A population of seeds grown from any seed in line 1 would be expected to have the same mean and variance as the parental generation.

8 (b) Genetic and environmental

(c) 350–800 mg (because the seed comes from line 3)

(d) 100–800 mg (because the seed might come from any of the three lines)

1.3 Inbreeding and outbreeding (related exercises 2.7, 2.8 and 3.1)

1 (a) Half

(b) Half of the white section should be shaded.

(c) One-sixteenth

2 (a) *Aa Bb cc Dd EE Ff* (b) 16

3 All of the alleles present in the gametes of the population.

4 (a) $q^2 = \frac{1}{2500}$, therefore q = 0.02

(b) 2pq = 0.039, i.e. approximately 4%

5 (a) *AA BB cc DD EE FF*

(b) *aa bb cc dd EE ff*

1.4 Measuring variation (related exercise 2.4)

1 (a) Environmental
  (b) a^1a b^1b c^1c d^1d e^1e
  (c) Environmental (because all the individuals, although heterozygous, are genetically identical)
  (d) 9
  (e) Genetic and environmental
2 $V_E = (4.29 + 22.97 + 14.64)/3 = 13.97$
3 $V_G = 50.68 - 13.97 = 36.71$
4 $36.71/50.68 = 0.72$

1.5 Heritability (related exercises 4.4 and 6.2)

1 V_G/V_P
2 (a) $65 - 2 = 63$ g (b) $65 + 3 = 68$ g
  (c) $65 + 2 + 3 = 70$ g
3 Litter number (pigs), egg hatchability (poultry) and number born (lambs) have low heritabilities.
4 (a) High (b) Low (c) 0 and 1
5 (a) 114 g
  (b) (i) 68.4 g (ii) $883 + 68.4 = 951.4$ g
  (c) (i) $951.4 + 55 = 1006.4$ g
     (ii) Heritability =

$$\frac{\text{selection response}}{\text{selection differential}} = \frac{55}{100} = 0.55$$

     (iii) As selection proceeds, the amount of genetic variation decreases.

Note: Heritabilities can also be expressed as percentages.
Source of data: H. L. Marks (1983) *Poultry Science* **62**:227–34 (adapted)

2 Selective breeding of plants and animals

2.1 Selection in sweet peas

1 Countess Spencer is pure breeding and therefore either homozygous recessive or homozygous dominant, assuming the two varieties differ at only a single gene locus. Prima Donna gave rise to Countess Spencer so is not necessarily pure breeding. Countess Spencer must be homozygous recessive.

2 A spontaneous mutation occurred once in Prima Donna and the new mutant allele was recessive to the allele giving the Prima Donna phenotype. The first plant carrying the new allele was heterozygous and so were some of its progeny. Heterozygous plants were distributed to different localities where self-fertilisation resulted in the production of homozygous recessive Countess Spencer.

3 The $3:1$ ratio in the F_2 generation suggests that the difference in colour is controlled by two alleles at a single gene locus with red dominant to pink. Countess Spencer is crossed to King Edward by removing the stamens from the flowers of one variety before the pollen has been shed. Pollen from the other variety is dusted onto the stigmas and the pollinated flowers are protected from further pollinations by covering with insect-proof bags. The reciprocal cross can also be done. The F_1 hybrids will have red flowers and plain standards. These are selfed and three-sixteenths of the progeny are expected to have red flowers and waved standards. All of these F_2 plants will be homozygous recessive for waved standards but may be heterozygous at the flower colour locus. The red, waved F_2 plants are again selfed. Any F_2 plant which does not produce pink progeny is likely to be homozygous dominant for red flowers. Its progeny should be pure breeding for both red flowers and waved standards.

2.2 Breeding tomatoes for resistance to eelworm

1 50%
2 $\frac{3}{4} = 75\%$

3 (a) $\frac{7}{8} = 87.5\%$ (b) $\frac{31}{32} = 96.875\%$
(c) $\frac{127}{128} = 99.22\%$

4 (a) 3 resistant : 1 susceptible
(b) One-third
(c) Self the resistant plants. Those which produce only resistant progeny are homozygous and so are all the progeny. The alternative method of testcrossing to the homozygous recessive is less satisfactory because all the offspring of the homozygous resistant will be heterozygous.

5 Nine years; one to produce F_1 + six for backcrosses + one to obtain homozygous plants + one to identify the homozygous plants. This method of transferring a single gene is called recurrent backcrossing. In the future, it may possibly be replaced by much quicker genetic engineering methods.

Source of data: P. R. Ellis and J. W. Maxon Smith (1971) *Euphytica* **20**:93–101

2.3 *Autosexing poultry and silkworms*

1 Males are $X^B X^b$ and females are $X^B Y$.

2 Males are $X^B X^b$ and $X^B X^B$. Females are $X^b Y$ and $X^B Y$.

3 (a) 50% brown and 50% yellow
(b) No

4 (a) XX ww
(b)

	Females' gametes	
Males' gametes all X	X	Y^w
	XX yellow (male)	XY^w brown (female)

5 In both poultry and silkworms autosexing relies on the action of a sex linked gene. In poultry it is X-linked and in silkworms it is Y-linked. In poultry the sex linked gene already existed in another breed but in silkworms there was no suitable gene so one was transferred to a sex chromosome by induced translocation. In poultry the colour difference is due to the presence of either one or two copies of an allele while in silkworms it is due to the presence or absence of an allele.

2.4 *Breeding cattle for milk (related exercises 1.1, 1.2 and 1.4)*

1 (a) The mean percentage butterfat of the F_1 cows falls between the means of the two parental breeds. The means of the backcross generations fall between the mean of the F_1 generation and the respective parental breed.
(b) Both genetic and environmental

2 (a) Some improvement may be possible because there will be some genetic variation present even though the breed has a history of inbreeding.
(b) Neither of the parental breeds is completely genetically uniform so there will be genetic variation in the F_1 generation. Even if there were no genetic variation in the parent breeds nor in the F_1 generation, segregation would give rise to genetic variation in the F_2 generation. By continued selection for increased butterfat percentage it should be possible to equal or even exceed the mean of the Jersey breed.

3 (a) Animals were less well fed during and soon after the two World Wars.
(b) Percentage butterfat is less susceptible to environmental factors than is milk yield.
(c) Increase in butterfat percentage is likely to be the result of a genetic change due to selection. It is less likely to be due to improved environmental conditions (see answer to 3(b)).

4 If there is no environmental variation then all the observed variation is genetic in origin. *Note*: In practice it is not possible to completely eliminate environmental variation so a bull's daughters are raised in several different herds and compared with their herdmates sired by different bulls. This is called the contemporary comparison method. In 1974 the UK Milk Marketing Board introduced the 'Improved Contemporary Comparison' (ICC) which takes into account the fact that most, if not all, cows in a herd will have been sired by selected bulls.

5 Milk is normally secreted only after the birth of a calf. However, about 80% of infertile cows can be induced to lactate by injection of oestrogen and prolactin.

6 (a) 2000
   (b) The probability that a daughter is heterozygous is $\frac{1}{2}$. The probability that a heterozygous daughter will produce a homozygous recessive calf by the bull is $\frac{1}{4}$. The proportion of homozygous recessive offspring is therefore

$$0.5 \times 0.25 = 0.125$$

2.5 The search for better soybeans

1 The protein would become denatured and therefore inactive.

2 Trypsin is a protease (an endopeptidase) produced in the pancreas of mammals.

3 Ingested protein would be inadequately digested and absorbed.

4 Hypothesis 1 is supported. If there were three different gene loci all producing SBTI we would expect to find many plants with more than one kind. The fact that none of the varieties had more than one SBTI would be consistent with hypothesis 2 only if two of the three loci in each plant produced no SBTI. We are told that such genes are rare. If hypothesis 1 is true, no plant can have more than two SBTIs and as the plants are all homozygous, they will have only one.

5 (a) The F_1 plants have both alleles and both are expressed.
   (b) 1 with one upper band : 2 with two bands : 1 with one lower band

6 $Ti^a Ti^a$ gives one band, $ti\ ti$ gives none. The F_1, $Ti^a ti$, gives one band in the same position as the $Ti^a Ti^a$ parent.

7 (a)

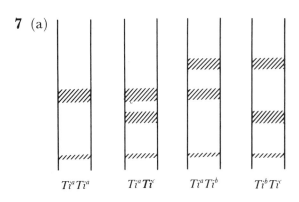

$Ti^a Ti^a$ $Ti^a Ti^c$ $Ti^a Ti^b$ $Ti^b Ti^c$

(b) $1:1:1:1$

Source of data: J. H. Orf and T. Hymowitz (1979) *Journal of the American Oil Chemists' Society* **56**:722–6

2.6 Breeding systems

1 Asexual progeny are produced by mitosis and so are genetically identical to the parent. Sexual reproduction involves the formation of genetically different gametes by meiosis and their subsequent fusion in fertilisation.

2 True statements are (i) A, E, F (ii) A, B, possibly E (see answer to question 3) (iii) B, C, D, F

3 A   Reproduction is possible if the parent plant is the only one growing or flowering in an area or is flowering when insect pollinators are not present.
   B   A mutant recessive allele which is potentially advantageous can become homozygous and so be expressed in the phenotype.
   C   The heterozygous offspring of a homozygous plant may show hybrid vigour. The effects of recessive alleles are hidden in heterozygotes and form a reserve of potentially useful genetic variation.
   D   Alleles at one gene locus may have different effects in different genetic backgrounds. Recombination allows selection of favourable epistatic interactions.

E In cross-fertilising species favourable gene combinations may be lost because of crossing over, reassortment of chromosomes and random fusion of gametes. Disruption of advantageous gene complexes may occur in self-fertilising species if the relevant gene loci are heterozygous but not if they are homozygous.

F A high level of heterozygosity may confer higher fitness as well as forming a reserve of genetic variation.

4 (a) Dioecious plants can only cross-fertilise. Examples are asparagus, date and spinach.

(b) In monoecious plants self-fertilisation is possible if there is no other mechanism to prevent it but physical separation of male and female flowers favours cross-pollination. Examples of monoecious plants are maize, chestnut, cucumber and melon.

(c) The close proximity of anthers and stigmas does not favour cross-pollination. In some species self-fertilisation occurs before the flowers open, e.g. lettuce, soya bean, wheat, barley, oats and rice.

(d) Protandry favours cross-fertilisation. However, where an individual plant bears several flowers at different stages of maturity, self-fertilisation is possible. Examples of protandrous crop plants are carrot, raspberry and maize.

(e) Smooth, light pollen grains are easily carried by wind to other plants but these characteristics of pollen do not necessarily favour cross-fertilisation. Wheat and barley have smooth, light pollen but are self-pollinated.

(f) The short life of pollen could favour either self- or cross-fertilisation. The life span of grass pollen is up to five hours. This means that in a protandrous species such as maize, most of a plant's own pollen is dead before the stigmas are mature. In other grasses the life span of pollen is only a few minutes and if the stigmas are receptive, self-fertilisation will be favoured.

2.7 Self-incompatibility in plants (related exercise 1.3)

1 s_1 and s_2

2

	Genotype of stigma				
Genotype of pollen parent	s_1s_2	s_1s_3	s_2s_3	s_2s_4	s_3s_4
s_1s_2	–	$\frac{1}{2}$	$\frac{1}{2}$	$\frac{1}{2}$	all
s_1s_3	$\frac{1}{2}$	–	$\frac{1}{2}$	all	$\frac{1}{2}$
s_2s_3	$\frac{1}{2}$	$\frac{1}{2}$	–	$\frac{1}{2}$	$\frac{1}{2}$
s_2s_4	$\frac{1}{2}$	all	$\frac{1}{2}$	–	$\frac{1}{2}$
s_3s_4	all	$\frac{1}{2}$	$\frac{1}{2}$	$\frac{1}{2}$	–

3 (a) s_1s_2 and s_2s_3
(b) s_1s_2 and s_1s_3
(c) s_1s_3, s_1s_4, s_2s_3 and s_2s_4

4 No. Where a certain allele occurs in the female plant, no male gamete with the same allele can fertilise one of its egg cells. (Sometimes incompatible pollen will grow a tube but very slowly. Plants homozygous for 'S' alleles can be obtained if competition from compatible pollen is prevented.)

5 The pollen which fertilised the egg cells must necessarily have come from a different variety so the seeds will be hybrid; they will not give rise to plants the same as the female parent variety.

6

	Genotype of stigma		
Genotype of pollen parent	s_1s_2	s_1s_3	s_2s_3
s_1s_2	–	–	s_1s_2, s_1s_3 s_2s_2, s_2s_3
s_1s_3	–	–	s_1s_2, s_1s_3 s_2s_3, s_3s_3

7 Yes

2.8 Hybrid corn (related exercise 1.3)

1 (a) *Gg Hh Jj Kk*
(b) *gg HH jj KK*
2 *Gg Hh Jj Kk*

3 $3^4 = 81$

4 Cross male sterile to inbred line and collect seed from male sterile. The progeny will have the male sterile cytoplasm and half the nuclear genes from each of the two parent lines. Cross the progeny to the inbred line and continue this backcrossing for about six generations (see exercise 2.2).

5 Hybrid corn with male sterile cytoplasm produces no viable pollen so the farmer would have to intersperse rows of hybrid corn with male fertile plants.

6 The male parent has *Rf/Rf* in the nucleus and normal cytoplasm. The female parent has *rf/rf* in the nucleus and male sterile cytoplasm. *Note:* For the production of male fertile offspring from a double cross, (A×B) × (C×D), A is cytoplasmic male sterile (cms), *rf/rf*; B is normal cytoplasm, *rf/rf*; C is cms, *rf/rf*; and D is normal cytoplasm, *Rf/Rf*. A×B progeny are cms, *rf/rf* (male sterile), and C×D progeny are cms, *Rf/rf* (male fertile). On crossing (A×B) × (C×D) the progeny are all cms but half are fertile because they are *Rf/rf* and provide enough pollen for fertilisation of all the progeny.

2.9 Polyploidy in crop plant evolution (related exercise 6.5)

1 (a) B

(b) C. Some cultivated clones have 22 *acuminata* + 11 *balbisiana* chromosomes. Others have 22 *balbisiana* + 11 *acuminata* chromosomes. Fruits develop parthenocarpically, i.e. without fertilisation, and the plants are propagated by means of corms.

(c) B

(d) A. *Fragaria virginiana* and *F. chiloensis* were both cultivated in Europe. *F. ananassa* appeared about 1750 as a fertile hybrid.

(e) D. The loganberry was discovered about 1881 by Judge Logan in his garden in California where both parental species were growing. The unreduced gamete came from the European raspberry, *R. idaeus*.

(f) B. All three species show a great deal of variation. Both the turnip and Chinese cabbage are *B. campestris*; cabbage, cauliflower, Brussels sprouts, kohlrabi and broccoli are *B. oleracea*; and *B. napus* gives us both the swede and oil-seed rape.

3 Resistance to pesticides
3.1 Resistance of flies to DDT (related exercises 1.1 and 1.3)

1 Hypothesis 2 describes a process of natural selection acting on already existing variation.

2 Hypothesis 2. The experiment was not designed to test hypothesis 1. Hypothesis 3 is not supported because selection was successful even though the flies exposed to DDT were not used for breeding. DDT could not have caused advantageous mutations to occur.

3 A

4 In each generation group A and group B flies are siblings and have 50% of their genes in common. If a particular group B shows resistance to DDT, its sibling group A is likely to carry the same genes. Selecting the group A flies with the most resistant siblings results in increasing the frequency of genes for resistance at each generation.

5 There was a limited amount of genetic variation affecting resistance present in the original population. By generation 7 all the alleles for resistance may have become homozygous (fixed). (The original flies were outbred and selecting a small number of them for breeding will cause inbreeding. The decrease in resistance in generations 1 and 2 may be due to inbreeding depression which causes a general reduction in fitness, including resistance. Although resistance subsequently improves due to selection for the appropriate genes, general fitness may remain depressed.)

Source of data: J. Bennett (1960) *Heredity* **15**:65–77 (adapted)

3.2 Dieldrin resistance in the Australian sheep blowfly (related exercises 3.5, 6.1 and 6.6)

1 The gradient shows the variation in lethal dose between flies within a strain: the steeper the gradient, the less the variation.

2 The F_1 flies are intermediate in resistance.

3 A dose of 0.1 µg dieldrin per fly would kill all flies with the genotype of the parental strain but none with the genotype of the F_1 generation.

4 If a single gene is responsible (*R* for resistance and *r* for susceptibility) then 50% of the backcross progeny would be *Rr* and 50% *rr*. The results support the hypothesis of single gene control because 50% are killed at a dose of 0.1 µg per fly but it takes 10 times as much dieldrin to kill the remaining 50%.

5 *RR* and *Rr* flies are resistant. In 1958–59, *RR* is 17.64% and *Rr* is 48.72%. Therefore the percentage of resistant flies is 66.36%. In 1972–73, *RR* is 0.16% and *Rr* is 7.68%. Therefore the percentage of resistant flies is 7.84%.

6 While flies are exposed to dieldrin, the resistance allele confers a selective advantage but when this insecticide is no longer present, the allele is disadvantageous compared with the allele for susceptibility.

Sources of data: G. J. Shanahan (1959) *Nature* **183**:1540–1; G. J. Shanahan (1961) *Genetica Agraria* **14**:307–21; J. W. Wright & R. Pal (eds.) (1967) *Genetics of insect vectors of disease*, Elsevier Publishing Co; J. A. Bishop & L. M. Cook (eds.) (1981) *Genetic consequences of man made change*, Academic Press

3.3 Herbicide resistance

1 (a) Evolution of herbicide resistance

involves a progressive increase in the frequency of the appropriate alleles in the gene pool. The allele frequency increases when the resistant plants contribute more offspring to the next generation than do the susceptible plants. The shorter the generation time, the more rapid the increase in the frequency of alleles promoting resistance.

(b) Self-fertilising species show a high degree of homozygosity. Any newly arising recessive mutant allele conferring resistance will become homozygous after one or two generations and so will be exposed to selection. In an outbreeding species, a recessive allele would have to reach a much higher frequency before homozygotes were produced. Resistance is often due to the combined effects of many genes. Plants which occasionally outbreed may gain benefit from the recombination of alleles at different loci and any new advantageous combinations will tend to be preserved due to the plant's habit of self-fertilisation.

(c) The weed *Stellaria media* has three generations per year and produces about 2000 seeds per plant. If all the seeds survive and reproduce, one plant could give rise to about 8×10^9 offspring in one year. Although mutation producing an allele for resistance is a rare event, the chance of getting one seed with a new mutant allele increases as the number of seeds increases.

2 (a) (i) 1 resistant : 1 susceptible
       (ii) 1 resistant : 1 susceptible
   (b) (i) All resistant (ii) All susceptible

3 Nursery A: 75 resistant. Nursery B: 100 resistant.

4 Nursery A: 2500 resistant progeny from 25 *RR* parents plus 50×75 resistant progeny from 50 *Rr* parents. Total 6250. Nursery B: $100 \times 100 = 10\,000$ resistant progeny.

5 (a) Seeds

(b) Seeds and pollen

6 (a) Maternal inheritance is advantageous because all offspring inherit resistance from their resistant mother. Resistant plants can rapidly colonise an area.

(b) Compared to chromosomal inheritance, maternal inheritance restricts the spread of the cytoplasmic factor to the agency of the seeds. Pollen carrying a chromosomal gene may be able to travel further afield.

3.4 The mechanisms of benomyl resistance in a fungus

1 Five alleles for resistance

2 (a) X (b) Z (c) Y

3 All the proteins move in the direction of the arrows. The mutant tubulin with an extra negative charge in strain 'X' moved further than the wild type tubulin so all the proteins were anions, moving towards the anode. For the proteins to have an overall negative charge, they have lost protons. This happens at a pH above the isoelectric point of the protein.

4 The general formula of an amino acid is $NH_2.R.CH.COOH$ and they can be conveniently divided into three categories. Amino acids which have no ionisable groups in the 'R' group are known as neutral. Those which have either a COOH or an NH_2 group in the 'R' group are acidic or basic respectively. A mutant tubulin will have the same charge as the wild type if one or more amino acids are substituted by amino acids in the same category.

5 One

6 Nine

7 If resistance to benomyl were conferred by one particular change within the gene for β-tubulin, a new resistance allele would occur very infrequently. In *Aspergillus nidulans* apparently many changes in the gene confer resistance. If the same is true in

disease-causing fungi it is not unlikely that one such mutation will occur within a few months of application of the fungicide to a wild population.

Source of data: G. Sheir-Neiss, M. H. Lai & N. R. Morris (1978) *Cell* **15**:639–47 (adapted)

3.5 Resistance of rodents to warfarin (related exercises 3.2, 6.1 and 6.6)

1 When the resistant male and his resistant progeny were crossed to susceptible rats, a ratio of 1 resistant : 1 susceptible was obtained. This ratio is consistent with variation at a single gene locus.

2 Heterozygous

3 Dominant

4 Recessive

5 Expected number of $Rw^1Rw^1 = 0.4356 \times 74 = 32$

Expected number of $Rw^1Rw^2 = 0.4488 \times 74 = 33$

Expected number of $Rw^2Rw^2 = 0.1156 \times 74 = 9$

(Expected values have been rounded to the nearest whole number and calculated using allele frequencies of 0·34 and 0·66.)

6 $\chi^2 = 5.31$ (calculated using unrounded expected values). The difference between observed and expected numbers is significant at below the 5% level of probability. Heterozygotes are more frequent than expected on the assumption of Hardy–Weinberg equilibrium.

7 Observed number of $Rw^1Rw^1 = 87·5\%$ of expected. Observed number of $Rw^2Rw^2 = 44\%$ of expected. Rw^2Rw^2 appears to be at the greatest disadvantage. This may be because Rw^2Rw^2 will have a constantly high vitamin K requirement while Rw^1Rw^1 rats are at a disadvantage only when they eat warfarin bait.

8 When the use of warfarin is stopped, Rw^1Rw^1 are no longer at a disadvantage, but Rw^2Rw^2 are. Because of a lack of vitamin K, they are more likely to die of internal haemorrhage and leave fewer offspring. The frequency of Rw^2 will diminish as the frequency of Rw^1 increases so the frequency of resistant rats declines.

Note: Warfarin is used as an anticoagulant drug in human medicine and it has been found that some people are resistant to its effects. Inheritance of resistance suggests an autosomal dominant gene is responsible.

Sources of data: J. H. Greaves, R. Redfern, P. B. Ayres & J. E. Gill (1977) *Genetical Research* **30**:257–63; M. E. Wallace & F. J. MacSwiney (1976) *Journal of Hygiene* **76**:173–81

4 Resistance to pests and diseases

4.1 Controlling powdery mildew of barley

1 $10^{13} \times 10^{-8} = 10^5$ spores/hectare day

2 (a) The more spores which are produced, the more likely it is that one carrying an appropriate mutant allele will reach a suitable site for germination.

(b) The haploid nature of the fungus means that any new mutant allele conferring virulence will be immediately expressed in the phenotype.

3 If a virulent pathogen infects one plant, neighbouring plants which are genetically identical will also be susceptible and will become infected when spores are released. There will be no resistant plants in the field and therefore no check to the outward wave of infection.

4 (a) 4.69 tonnes/hectare

(b) 5.07 tonnes/hectare   (c) 8.1%

(d) Average yield in monoculture = $(4.78 + 4.63 + 4.71)/3 =$ 4.71 tonnes/hectare.

Yield of these three cultivars in a

mixture would be $4.71 \times 1.081 =$ 5.09 tonnes/hectare.

Source of data: M. S. Wolfe & J. A. Barrett (1980) *Plant Disease* **64**: 148–55

4.2 Resistance to fungal diseases in rubber and tobacco (related exercise 1.2)

2 Variation in resistance could be genetic or environmental or, most likely, both.

3 One. Variation in the resistant inbred strain shows that resistance is susceptible to environmental influences. The distribution in the F_2 generation could be interpreted as showing a ratio of 3 resistant : 1 susceptible but the distinction between the categories is not clear cut owing to environmental variation.

Sources of data: N. W. Simmonds (1979) *Principles of crop improvement*, Longman; N. W. Simmonds (1983) *FAO Plant Protection Bulletin* **31**

4.3 Resistance of rice to whitebacked planthopper

1 3 resistant : 1 susceptible

2 One

3 Two-thirds

4 B and a are alleles for susceptibility and b is an allele for resistance. $\frac{1}{16}$ are $aa\ BB$ and $\frac{2}{16}$ are $aa\ Bb$. These $\frac{3}{16}$ are susceptible.

5 $\frac{6}{13}$. None of the F_3 families from selfed F_2 plants having AA or bb will be segregating families. Selfed $Aa\ BB$ and $Aa\ Bb$ F_2 plants will have some susceptible progeny.

Source of data: R. N. Nair, T. M. Masajo and G. S. Khush (1982) *Theoretical and Applied Genetics* **61**:19–22

4.4 Resistance of cotton to pests (related exercise 1.5)

1 The greater the seedling gossypol content, the less the damage.

2 (a) *GG HH* has 0.73% and *Gg HH* has 0.60%. These would be the same if *G* were completely dominant to *g*. (A similar comparison could be made between *GG hh* and *Gg hh*.)

(b) *GG HH* has 0.73% and *GG Hh* has 0.57%. These would be the same if *H* were completely dominant to *h*. (A similar comparison could be made between *gg HH* and *gg Hh*.)

3 (a) (0.13 + 0.11)/2 = 0.12%

(b) (0.42 + 0.28 + 0.38)/3 = 0.36%

(c) (0.57 + 0.6)/2 = 0.585%

5 The weight of pupae raised on a gossypol medium was lower than that of the controls for the first three generations.

6 The caterpillars are resistant to gossypol in their diet.

7 2% is over twice the percentage of gossypol in the *GG HH* plants. Even if plants with such high levels could be bred, the selection experiment shows that resistance in the moth would evolve very quickly.

8 There is already genetic variation for gossypol resistance in the wild population of *Heliothis*.

Sources of data: F. D. Wilson & T. N. Shaver (1973) *Crop Science* **13**:107–10; J. R. Raulston, D. A. Wolfenbarger & A. C. Bartlett (1985) *Journal of Economic Entomology* **78**:158–62

4.5 Myxomatosis in Australian rabbits

1 The virus is carried by mosquitoes which breed in water.

2 Genetically determined resistance should give life-long protection against myxomatosis and is heritable. Passive acquired immunity protects for a short period after birth and is not heritable in the Mendelian sense.

3 The virus had been stored at low temperature since 1953. Its virulence may have been reduced by the conditions of storage.

4 The variable being measured is resistance in rabbits and so the virulence of the virus should be constant. It would not be appropriate to use viruses freshly isolated from the wild each year because their virulence was also changing.

5 Evolution occurs by natural selection amongst genetically variable progeny. The more frequently progeny are produced, the greater the rate of evolution.

6 Mosquitoes feed on many different rabbits, so a virus which allows its host to live will be passed on to many other hosts. There is less disadvantage to virulence when the vector is a flea because fleas bite fewer hosts than mosquitoes do. While the host remains alive its fleas tend to stay with it so the less virulent viruses are less likely to be passed on. Fleas leave a dead host so virulent viruses are more likely to be carried by fleas seeking new hosts. (Observations on rabbits suggest that resistance to myxomatosis could be partly due to altered behaviour. Fleas tend to transfer between hosts in the nest, so rabbits that remain above ground are less likely to be bitten by fleas from another rabbit.)

Sources of data: C. H. Andrewes, H. V. Thompson & W. Mansi (1959) *Nature* **184**:1179–80; F. Fenner (1959) *British Medical Bulletin* **15**:240–5; H. V. Thompson (1954) *Annals of Applied Biology* **41**:358–66

5 New techniques for gene manipulation

5.1 Drug resistance in bacteria

1 Hypothesis 2. Antibiotic resistant bacteria were present on the original plate even though they had not been exposed to antibiotic (see also exercise 3.1). Resistant

E. coli have been isolated from the faeces of people living in remote places who have never been administered antibiotics.

2 The replica-plates would have similar numbers of colonies as the original plate.

3 As a reference point from which to locate the antibiotic resistant colonies on the original plate.

4 No colonies would grow on the plate. The penicillin would kill the streptomycin resistant and the streptomycin would kill the penicillin resistant bacteria.

5 (a) If the rate of mutation to resistance for each drug is 10^{-7}, the probability that one cell will simultaneously acquire, by mutation, resistance to both antibiotics is $10^{-7} \times 10^{-7} = 10^{-14}$.

(b) The bacteria which are not killed by one antibiotic will be killed by the other. The answer to 5 (a) shows that acquisition of resistance to both antibiotics, by mutation, is very unlikely.

(c) There are 1.678×10^7 after 8 hours.

6 Continual exposure of normal symbionts in the gut to antibiotics will select for R plasmids. These can be transferred by conjugation to pathogenic bacteria either in the gut or in sewage.

7 Calves are exposed to antibiotics to a much greater extent than are humans. If the human were on a course of antibiotics there would be selection in favour of the 0.02% resistant bacteria already in residence and the proportion would rise.

8 If antibiotics are used extensively in animal husbandry for disease prevention and growth promotion, the consequent selection of antibiotic resistant strains of bacteria means that the same antibiotics will be ineffective in the treatment of human disease caused by these bacteria.

5.2 Protein synthesis

1 The process of transcription involves breakage of the hydrogen bonds holding together the two strands of the double helix of DNA. One of the exposed DNA strands acts as a template for the synthesis of messenger RNA. Ribonucleotide precursors (ribonucleoside triphosphates) form hydrogen bonds through their bases to complementary bases on the DNA. As each ribonucleotide comes into position it is joined through its phosphate group to the growing sugar-phosphate backbone.

2 1 cytosine; 2 adenine; 3 guanine; 4 adenine; 5 uracil

3 RNA polymerase.

4 F, C, B, K, G, E, A, J, D, I, H or K, G, E, F, C, B, A, J, D, I, H

5 (a) TAC (b) UAC

6 In sentences A, J and K

7 (a) Base pairing allows accurate DNA replication.

(b) Base pairing permits the information in DNA to be copied precisely and carried to the ribosomes for protein synthesis.

8 The correspondence of the base sequence in nucleic acids to the amino acid sequence in a polypeptide. It is a triplet code where three bases in DNA (and mRNA) specify a particular amino acid.

9 (a) Anticodon, codon and ribosome binding site are in RNA; intron and promoter are in DNA.

(b) Anticodon, three adjacent unpaired bases in a tRNA molecule which are complementary to a codon in mRNA. Codon, three adjacent bases in an mRNA molecule which code for a specific amino acid or for polypeptide chain termination. Intron, a non-coding sequence of bases found between coding sequences in some genes of eukaryotes. Promoter, a sequence of bases in DNA which is recognised by RNA polymerase as the site to begin transcription. Ribosome binding site, a sequence of bases on mRNA by which the molecule binds to a ribosome.

10

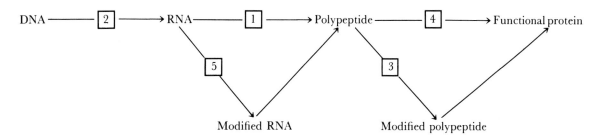

5.3 Recombinant DNA methods I. Cutting and joining DNA

Note: Bam HI, *Eco* RI and *Hin*d III are pronounced Bam H one, Eco R one and Hin D three.

1 The recognition sequence is, in each case, a palindrome.

Pst I	...C T G C A G...
	...G A C G T C...
Sst I	...G A G C T C...
	...C T C G A G...
Kpn I	...G G T A C C...
	...C C A T G G...

2 7×10^5 pieces

3 Restriction endonucleases which cut DNA at specific recognition sites; DNA ligase which seals gaps in the sugar phosphate backbone of DNA; reverse transcriptase which makes a DNA transcript of RNA.

5.4 Recombinant DNA methods II. Transformation and selection

1 $191 \times 3 = 573$ base pairs

2 The coding region may be interrupted by introns and there are control regions 'upstream' of the coding region.

3 In the genetic code, the first two bases of the codon are critical but the third base is variable. The function of a gene probe is to stick to its complementary sequence on the nitrocellulose paper. As the greatest adhesion occurs between exactly complementary strands, a number of probes are synthesised, having all possible combinations of bases at the third position of each triplet.

4 1 or 2, B or D; 3, L; 4, C; 5, J; 6, F; 7, 8 or 9, A, E or M; 10, H; 11, K; 12, G.

5 (a) Grow the bacteria first on tetracycline medium, then on ampicillin medium.

(b) *Pst* I cuts pBR322 in the gene for resistance to ampicillin. Growing cells first on tetracycline medium finds cells that have been transformed by a plasmid. Growing these on ampicillin medium finds the cells that have been transformed by a recombinant plasmid (by replica-plating).

5.5 Recombinant DNA in perspective

1 Paragraph 1 refers to the human body recognising animal insulin as a foreign substance and making antibodies against it. Paragraph 4 refers to animals responding to infection and vaccines by making antibodies. Paragraph 5 mentions the use of monoclonal antibodies to extract pure antigen from a mixture.

3 *Notes:* Transferring single genes ((i), (ii) and (vi)) should be possible. The growth rate of mice has already been increased by transferring into them genes for rat growth hormone; perhaps the same will be done for cattle. There is concern that (i) could be used to create a pathogen for germ warfare but there are plenty of pathogens already available. A bacterial gene for glyphosate resistance has been introduced into tobacco. Glyphosate is an indiscriminate herbicide used for ground clearance but it could be used as a selective herbicide if the crop could be made resistant to it. It is unlikely that cereals could be given genes for nitrogen fixation but it is probably more feasible to genetically engineer cereals so that they can form symbioses with root nodule bacteria. It is unlikely that sufficient will ever be known about the genetic control of human behaviour or animals' limb development to make these characters the subject of genetic engineering.

4 *Notes:* Most of these points are a matter of opinion. Genes naturally cross species boundaries, e.g. in plant hybridisation, in conjugation between different species of bacteria and in infection of plants by *Agrobacterium tumefaciens*. Any monster, dangerous or not, would have much too complex a genetic architecture to be created accidentally.

6 Human variation

6.1 Geographical variation in blood groups (related exercises 3.2, 3.5 and 6.6)

1 31.36%

2 pq(I^0I^A),   q^2(I^AI^A),   qr(I^AI^B),   pr(I^0I^B), qr(I^AI^B), r^2(I^BI^B)

3

| | I^0I^0 | I^0I^A | I^0I^B | I^AI^A | I^AI^B | I^BI^B |
	%	%	%	%	%	%
(a)	43.56	42.24	2.64	10.24	1.28	0.04
(b)	37.21	19.52	28.06	2.56	7.36	5.29
(c)	94.09	3.88	1.94	0.04	0.04	0.01

4

	A	B	O	AB
(a)	52.48%	2.68%	43.56%	1.28%
(b)	22.08%	33.35%	37.21%	7.36%
(c)	3.92%	1.95%	94.09%	0.04%

Note: Allele I^0 may also be called *i*.

6.2 Continuous variation (related exercises 1.1, 1.2 and 1.5)

1 Both genetic and environmental differences

2 The sex difference is genetic in origin. Women are generally smaller than men and so one would expect their fingers to be shorter. But the difference could be a consequence of the fact that the two samples are not independent. The means of the samples would differ as observed if one of the factors in the choice of a marriage partner were that the man is taller than the woman (and therefore has bigger hands). In fact the original data give a correlation coefficient of 0.4 between mothers' and fathers' finger lengths.

3 D

6.3 A question of paternity

1 (a) Baby X
   (b) Baby X can only be assigned to Mr and Mrs T by elimination. Mrs S transmits only L^M so cannot have a group N child.

2 (a) AB or M (b) O or B or M or Rhesus negative

3 (a) 0.03 (only AB is excluded)
   (b) 0.2 (father cannot be group N)
   (c) 0 (a Rhesus positive or negative man could be the father)
   (d) 0.55 (father cannot be O or B)

4 Rhesus positive and MN

5 (a) B and E
   (b) G
   (c) F and I

6.4 Self and non-self

1 (a) 210 (b) 820 (c) 36 (d) 78

2 483 537 600

3 (a) Eight (b) Seven

4 (a) (i) One-quarter   (ii) Three-quarters
    (iii) One-quarter
  (b) (i) Three   (ii) Four
  (c) A sister with the same genotype as the
    son would be the ideal choice. The
    mother or a sister with the haplotypes
    A2 C1 B13 D6 and *A3 C6 B27 D3* have
    only three antigens different from the
    son so either would be the next best
    choice. The father and a sister with the
    haplotypes *A2 C3 B5 D2* and *A3 C6 B27
    D3* have four different antigens and the
    least suitable donor would be a sister
    with the haplotypes *A3 C6 B27 D3* and
    A2 C1 B13 D6 who has seven different
    antigens.

6.5 Chromosome abnormalities (related exercise 2.9)

1 (a) 1 (b) 0.5
2 There will be three different chromosomes
  21 if non-disjunction occurs at the first
  meiotic division. If non-disjunction occurs
  at the second division in the mother, the
  two chromosomes 21 inherited from her
  will be exact replicas except for regions
  exchanged with the other homologue in
  crossing over during prophase I.
3 (a) XXY, XXX, X0 (X from father) and
    Y0
  (b) XXY, XXX X0 (X from father) and
    Y0
4 (a) XXY and X0 (X from mother)
  (b) XXX (two of the X-chromosomes
    identical) and XYY (the two Y-
    chromosomes are identical)
  Note: The commonly used possessive
  'Down's syndrome', 'Turner's syndrome'
  etc. are being replaced by the non-posses-
  sive 'Down syndrome', 'Turner syndrome'
  etc.

6.6 Genetics and malaria (related exercises 3.2, 3.5 and 6.1)

1 (a) (i) 810 (ii) 180 (iii) 10

  (b) 0.1
  (c) 180/1980 = 0.091
  (d) 648 *BB* and 180 *Bb* remain. The
    frequency of allele *b* is 180/1656 =
    0.1087
2 A stable polymorphism would be maintained if as many *B* alleles are removed by
  failure of homozygotes to reproduce as a
  result of malaria as *b* alleles are removed by
  death from thalassaemia.
3 The frequency of alleles for β-thalassaemia
  should decline if there is no heterozygous
  advantage but the decline will be slow
  because most of the alleles are in heterozygotes. However, a decline in frequency will
  not necessarily occur now that carriers can
  be identified and the disease can be diagnosed prenatally. If heterozygous parents choose to abort thalassaemic foetuses,
  they may have only phenotypically normal
  children, two-thirds of whom will be carriers.

6.7 Single gene disorders

1 A or C. It is commonly stated that the
  mutation must have occurred in Queen
  Victoria herself, but to have affected her
  germ cells, it must have occurred during
  mitosis early in her foetal life.
2 In A two normal parents have had affected
  children and there is no evidence that the
  disease is sex linked. The autosomal recessive disease given is cystic fibrosis. In B the
  disease occurs in every generation except
  the last. The autosomal dominant disease
  given is Huntington's disease (Huntington's chorea). Any individuals in generation IV are too young to show symptoms.
  In C only males are affected and inheritance shows a sex linked pattern. The sex
  linked condition given is Duchenne muscular dystrophy.
3 (a) 0.67
  (b) 0.5
  (c) 0.043 (1/23) because this is the

frequency of heterozygotes in the general population.

4 (a) 0.5
  (b) II-9 was almost certainly heterozygous because her daughter, III-13, had Huntington's disease.
  (c) The probability that III-4 is heterozygous is 0.5. If he is heterozygous, the probability is 0.7 that he would not be showing symptoms. The probability that he is heterozygous but not showing symptoms is therefore $0.5 \times 0.7 = 0.35$.

5 (a) II-2 is almost certainly heterozygous because her daughter III-5 is also heterozygous.
  (b) (i) 0.5

(ii) Foetal skin cells removed by amniocentesis are inspected for the presence of a Barr body (an inactivated X-chromosome). Cells with two X-chromosomes have one Barr body and cells with an X- and a Y-chromosome have none.

  (c) (i) II-2 is a carrier so the probability that III-2 is a carrier is 0.5. If III-2 is a carrier then the probability of IV-2 being a carrier is 0.5. The probability that IV-2 is a carrier is therefore $0.5 \times 0.5 = 0.25$.
    (ii) If she is a carrier, the probability that a son will be affected is 0.5. Therefore the probability that IV-2's son will be affected is $0.25 \times 0.5 = 0.125$.

Index